Understanding Eating Disorders

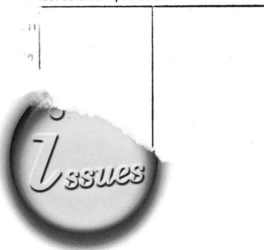

Volume 184

Series Editor

Lisa Firth

 *Independence*

Educational Publishers
Cambridge

First published by Independence
The Studio, High Green
Great Shelford
Cambridge CB22 5EG
England

British Library Cataloguing in Publication Data
Understanding Eating Disorders — (Issues; v.184)
1. Eating disorders 2. Body image 3. Obesity
I. Series II. Firth, Lisa
616.8'526-dc22

ISBN-13: 978 1 86168 525 4

Printed in Great Britain
MWL Print Group Ltd

Cover
The illustration on the front cover is by
Simon Kneebone.

CONTENTS

Useful information for readers

Dear Reader,

Issues: Understanding Eating Disorders

It is common for young people to worry about their weight, size and shape, and in some people this may develop into an eating disorder such as anorexia or bulimia. Although these disorders are most common in young women, men are increasingly affected, as are older people. An NHS survey in 2007 found that an alarming 6.4% of adults over 16 had a problem with food. This book examines types of eating disorder, what causes them and how they can best be tackled.

The purpose of *Issues*

Understanding Eating Disorders is the one hundred and eighty-fourth volume in the **Issues** series. The aim of this series is to offer up-to-date information about important issues in our world. Whether you are a regular reader or new to the series, we do hope you find this book a useful overview of the many and complex issues involved in the topic. This title replaces an older volume in the **Issues** series, Volume 127: **Eating Disorders** which is now out of print.

Titles in the **Issues** series are resource books designed to be of especial use to those undertaking project work or requiring an overview of facts, opinions and information on a particular subject, particularly as a prelude to undertaking their own research.

The information in this book is not from a single author, publication or organisation; the value of this unique series lies in the fact that it presents information from a wide variety of sources, including:

⇨ Government reports and statistics
⇨ Newspaper articles and features
⇨ Information from think-tanks and policy institutes
⇨ Magazine features and surveys
⇨ Website material
⇨ Literature from lobby groups and charitable organisations.*

Critical evaluation

Because the information reprinted here is from a number of different sources, readers should bear in mind the origin of the text and whether the source is likely to have a particular bias or agenda when presenting information (just as they would if undertaking their own research). It is hoped that, as you read about the many aspects of the issues explored in this book, you will critically evaluate the information presented. It is important that you decide whether you are being presented with facts or opinions. Does the writer give a biased or an unbiased report? If an opinion is being expressed, do you agree with the writer?

Understanding Eating Disorders offers a useful starting point for those who need convenient access to information about the many issues involved. However, it is only a starting point. Following each article is a URL to the relevant organisation's website, which you may wish to visit for further information.

Kind regards,

Lisa Firth
Editor, **Issues** series

** Please note that Independence Publishers has no political affiliations or opinions on the topics covered in the **Issues** series, and any views quoted in this book are not necessarily those of the publisher or its staff.*

ISSUES TODAY
A RESOURCE FOR KEY STAGE 3

Younger readers can also benefit from the thorough editorial process which characterises the **Issues** series with our resource books for 11- to 14-year-old students, **Issues Today**. In addition to containing information from a wide range of sources, rewritten with this age group in mind, **Issues Today** titles also feature comprehensive glossaries, an accessible and attractive layout and handy tasks and assignments which can be used in class, for homework or as a revision aid. In addition, these titles are fully photocopiable. For more information, please visit our website (www.independence. co.uk).

Eating disorders in young people

For parents, carers and anyone who works with young people

What are eating disorders?

Worries about weight, shape and eating are common, especially among young girls. Being very overweight or obese can cause a lot of problems, particularly with health. Quite often, someone who is overweight can lose weight simply by eating more healthily. It sounds easy, but they may need help to find a way of doing this.

A lot of young people, many of whom are not overweight in the first place, want to be thinner. They often try to lose weight by dieting or skipping meals. For some, worries about weight become an obsession. This can turn into a serious eating disorder. This factsheet is about the most common eating disorders – anorexia nervosa and bulimia nervosa.

⇨ Someone with anorexia nervosa worries all the time about being fat (even if they are skinny) and eats very little. They lose a lot of weight and their periods become irregular or stop.

⇨ Someone with bulimia nervosa also worries a lot about weight. They alternate between eating next to nothing, and then having binges when they gorge themselves. They vomit or take laxatives to control their weight.

Both of these eating disorders are more common in girls, but do occur in boys. They can happen in young people of all backgrounds and cultures.

What are the signs of anorexia or bulimia?

⇨ Weight loss or unusual weight changes.

⇨ Periods being irregular or stopping.

⇨ Missing meals, eating very little and avoiding 'fattening' foods.

⇨ Avoiding eating in public, secret eating.

⇨ Large amounts of food disappearing from the cupboards.

⇨ Believing they are fat when underweight.

⇨ Exercising excessively, often in secret.

⇨ Becoming preoccupied with food, cooking for other people, calorie counting and setting target weights.

⇨ Going to the bathroom or toilet immediately after meals.

⇨ Using laxatives and vomiting to control weight or sometimes other medications/herbal remedies to lose weight.

It may be difficult for parents or teachers to tell the difference between ordinary dieting in young people and a more serious problem. If you are concerned about your child's weight and how they are eating, consult your GP. You can also seek help and advice from other agencies (see sources of further information at the end of this article).

What effects can eating disorders have?

⇨ Feeling excessively cold.

⇨ Headaches and dizziness.

⇨ Changes in hair and skin.

⇨ Tiredness and difficulty with normal activities.

⇨ Damage to health, including stunting of growth and damage to bones and internal organs.

⇨ Loss of periods and risk of infertility.

⇨ Anxiety and depression.

⇨ Poor concentration, missing school, college or work.

⇨ Lack of confidence, withdrawal from friends.

⇨ Dependency or over-involvement with parents, instead of developing independence.

It's important to remember that, if allowed to continue unchecked, both anorexia and bulimia can be

life-threatening conditions. Over time, they are harder to treat, and the effects become more serious.

What causes eating disorders?

Eating disorders are caused by a number of different things:

⇨ Worry or stress may lead to comfort eating. This may cause worries about getting fat.

⇨ Dieting and missing meals lead to craving for food, loss of control and over-eating.

⇨ Anorexia or bulimia can develop as a complication of more extreme dieting, perhaps triggered by an upsetting event, such as family breakdown, death or separation in the family, bullying at school or abuse.

⇨ Sometimes, anorexia and bulimia may be a way of trying to feel in control if life feels stressful.

⇨ More ordinary events, such as the loss of a friend, a teasing remark or school exams, may also be the trigger in a vulnerable person.

Risk factors

Risk factors include:

⇨ being female;
⇨ being previously overweight;
⇨ lacking self-esteem;
⇨ being perfectionistic.

Obsessional behaviour is often seen in young people with eating disorders.

Sensitive or anxious individuals who are having difficulty becoming independent from their families are also more at risk. Eating disorders can also run in families. The families of young people with eating disorders often find change or conflict particularly difficult, and may be unusually close or over-protective.

Where can I get help?

If you think a young person may be developing an eating disorder, don't be afraid to ask them if they are worried about themselves. Quite often young people with eating disorders are unable to acknowledge there may be a problem, and will not want you to interfere and may become angry or upset.

However, you may still be worried and you can seek advice from

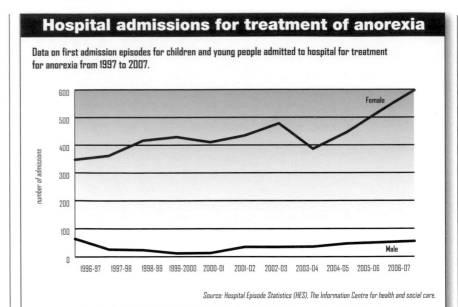

Hospital admissions for treatment of anorexia

Data on first admission episodes for children and young people admitted to hospital for treatment for anorexia from 1997 to 2007.

Source: Hospital Episode Statistics (HES), The Information Centre for health and social care.

professionals in different agencies, e.g. GP, Child and Adolescent Mental Health Services (CAMHS). It is important that you feel supported and not alone.

These simple suggestions are useful to help young people to maintain a healthy weight and avoid eating disorders.

⇨ Eat regular meals – The British Dietetic Association recommends eating regularly throughout the day, which usually means three main meals and three nutritious snacks in between such as fruit, yogurt or nuts. Too many sugary or high-fat snacks should be avoided.

⇨ Try to eat a 'balanced' diet – one that contains all the types of food your body needs, including carbohydrate foods such as bread, rice, pasta or cereals with every meal.

⇨ Don't miss meals – long gaps encourage overeating.

⇨ Take regular exercise.

⇨ Try not to be influenced by other people skipping meals or commenting on weight.

When professional help is needed

When eating problems make family meals stressful, it is important to seek professional advice. Your GP will be able to advise you about what specialist help is available locally and will be able to arrange a referral. This will usually be to the local CAMHS.

Working with the family is an important part of treatment

If the eating disorder causes physical ill health, it is essential to get medical help quickly. Eating disorders can have very serious long-term consequences, but if the young person receives help from a specialist early on, they have a better chance of a healthier outcome.

Recommended reading

⇨ *The Mind: A User's Guide*: Editor Raj Persaud, Bantam Press, 2007.

⇨ *The Young Mind: An essential guide to mental health for young adults, parents and teachers*, Bantam Press, 2009.

Sources of further information

⇨ B-EAT: Adult Helpline 0845 634 1414; Youth Helpline 0845 634 7650; textphone service 01603 753322;

⇨ YoungMinds provides information and advice on child mental health issues. Parents' Information Service 0800 018 2138.

Revised December 2009
Series editor: Dr Mona Freeman
Editorial Board: Child and Family Public Education Editorial Board.

⇨ The above information is re-printed with kind permission from the Royal College of Psychiatrists. Visit www.rcpsych.ac.uk for more information on this and other related topics.

© *Royal College of Psychiatrists*

Anorexia

Information from the BMJ Publishing Group

What is it?

Anorexia is a condition that leads to problems with eating. Its full name is anorexia nervosa. If you have anorexia, you're very underweight and you dread being fat.

Having anorexia means you think you are fat even when you are very thin. You often go to a lot of trouble to avoid eating. You may also make yourself throw up, take laxatives or spend hours exercising.

Having anorexia means you think you are fat even when you are very thin. You often go to a lot of trouble to avoid eating

---

If you have anorexia, you may not understand the way you behave. You may feel ashamed and guilty about it but tell yourself there's nothing wrong. But anorexia is harmful. You can die from starving yourself.

Getting help is very important. Admitting you have a problem is the first, yet hardest, step. If you take that step, you can find the support and treatment you need to stop anorexia taking over your life.

Key points for people with anorexia

⇨ Anorexia is a serious medical condition, not just a phase or a fad.
⇨ If you have anorexia, you may not be able to admit you have a problem. And you may not want treatment.
⇨ You dread getting fat. And you think you are fat even when you are much too thin and weigh too little for your height.
⇨ Having anorexia seriously damages your health. It makes you starve your body of the food it needs to work properly.

⇨ It is possible to get better. You can put on weight and keep it on. And you can change how you think about weight and food. But it's not easy.
⇨ Most people think of anorexia as something women get. But men can get it too.

What's normal eating?

It's hard to say what 'normal eating' is. A lot more has been written about what's not normal.

Usually, eating normally means you eat when you feel hungry and stop when you feel full. These feelings are partly controlled by chemicals in your brain. Most of us eat three meals a day, with a couple of snacks in between.

Food plays a big part in most of our lives. We spend a lot of time shopping for and preparing food. When we meet friends or relatives, we often eat together. How do we decide what to eat? We make choices because of our lifestyle and attitudes toward food and health, but also because of what tastes good.

Some people think about food or their body size more than others. Many people, especially women, worry about their weight and try to control how much they eat. Sharing food with family and friends is part of normal, healthy eating.

But whether we think about food a lot or a little, worry about it or just enjoy it, our feelings about food

don't usually stop us from living a normal life.

What goes wrong in anorexia?

If you have anorexia, you worry about food and your weight a lot more than most people do.
⇨ You are frightened about getting fat.
⇨ You think you are fat, and you think other people think you are too.
⇨ You spend most of your time thinking about how much you weigh and how you look. You become obsessed with losing weight.
⇨ Fear of putting on weight is part of having anorexia. You may have other fears too. You may fear losing control. You probably worry about other people finding out that you have anorexia. You may be afraid of being told that you have a mental health problem.

These kinds of thoughts and worries go round and round in your head.

Here's a list of some things you may do if you have anorexia. You may:
⇨ Miss meals or avoid eating, even when you feel hungry;
⇨ Hide food or keep a lot of it around (hoard it);
⇨ Cut your food up into tiny pieces and push it around your plate to look as though you've eaten some;
⇨ Avoid eating with others;
⇨ Deny that you have a problem with food;
⇨ Carefully weigh your food and only eat small quantities;
⇨ Get rid of the calories you've eaten by making yourself throw up or by taking laxatives;
⇨ Do other things to lose weight, such as exercising more than is healthy;
⇨ Check your weight all the time and examine your body in the mirror (especially your tummy, thighs and bottom);

⇨ Worry about your weight so much that you don't have time for studying, working or socialising. The rest of your life can start to fall apart.

But anorexia is not just about how you feel about food. It's also about how you feel about yourself. A person with anorexia is terrified of being fat, even when their weight is normal.

If you have anorexia, you can't see that you are very underweight. You may feel deeply unhappy.

Starving yourself can seem like a way to control difficult emotions and stress. You may think that losing weight is the key to a better, happier and more successful life.

Anorexia is a real and serious illness. It's not a diet that's gone wrong or a fad. It's one of the group of illnesses called eating disorders, along with bulimia and binge-eating.

If you think you have problems with food, there are some questions you can ask yourself. These are the questions doctors use to help them decide if you have an eating disorder.

Why me?

There's no simple reason why someone gets anorexia, and we don't know what causes eating disorders. It's probably a combination of the genes you're born with and the things that happen in your life that lead to anorexia. Here's a list of some of the things that have been linked to anorexia.

⇨ Emotional problems;
⇨ Dieting;
⇨ Wanting to look like models on television and in magazines;
⇨ An imbalance of chemicals in the brain;
⇨ Genes and family history.

Some people are more likely to get anorexia than others. Things that can increase your chances of getting an illness are called risk factors. The risk factors for anorexia include:

⇨ Having low self-esteem (thinking you are worthless and not giving yourself any credit when things go well);
⇨ Wanting to be perfect as a child and always doing exactly what you're told;
⇨ Having mental health problems such as depression, anxiety or an obsessive way of thinking;
⇨ Being competitive.

9 February 2009

⇨ The above information is reprinted with kind permission from the BMJ Publishing Group. Visit www.bmj.com for more information or to view references for this article.

Bulimia

Information from the BMJ Publishing Group

What is it?

If you have bulimia, you worry about putting on weight. But you sometimes lose control and eat huge amounts of food. Afterwards you might make yourself sick, take medicines such as laxatives or water pills, or exercise intensely so as not to gain weight. You keep all of this secret, and you might feel ashamed and guilty.

In developed countries, around one to two in every 200 young women have bulimia. Men can have bulimia too, but it's much more common in women. For every man who has the condition, there are around nine or ten women who have it.

If you have bulimia, you might tell yourself it's not important. But bulimia is serious. It can damage your health.

In developed countries, around one to two in every 200 young women have bulimia

---

If you get help, the chances are good that you can get rid of bulimia. And the earlier you get help, the better your chances of making a full recovery. Admitting you have a problem is the hardest step. But once you do, there are treatments that can make you feel better and help you eat in a healthy way again.

Key points for people with bulimia

⇨ More than three people in every 100 have an eating problem like bulimia at some point in their life.
⇨ It's very hard for people with bulimia to ask for help, so they often keep their illness secret for years.
⇨ Symptoms vary from one person to another. If your symptoms don't fit the exact definition for bulimia, you may still have an eating disorder. Treatments for bulimia can also help people with other eating disorders.
⇨ If you get treatment, you have a good chance of getting better. And the earlier you seek help, the better that chance will be.

⇨ Even if you've had bulimia for a long time, getting treatment can help you eat in a healthy way again.

If you have bulimia, you might also have had another eating disorder called anorexia. People who have anorexia sometimes get bulimia. These two diseases are closely linked.

Sharing food with family is a normal part of healthy eating and should be fun.

Healthy eating

If you eat in a healthy way, you eat when you're hungry and stop when you're full. Most of us tend to eat three meals a day with perhaps a couple of snacks in between.

Eating is also usually a pleasure. When we meet up with family and friends, we often eat together. It's something most people look forward to and enjoy.

What goes wrong?

If you have bulimia, you worry about food and your body shape far more than most people do. You are horrified by the thought of being fat or getting fat. You think all the time about how you look and how much you weigh.

These feelings lead to irregular, unhealthy eating habits like the ones listed below.

⇨ You think about food all the time. You count calories, plan what you'll eat, and worry about meals.

⇨ Sometimes you lose control and binge, eating large amounts at one time, in secret.

⇨ Afterwards you might try to get rid of the calories you've just eaten by purging (throwing up or using laxatives or water pills).

⇨ Or you might try to avoid putting on weight by not eating for a long time or by exercising obsessively.

⇨ Vomiting or using laxatives can make your stomach feel empty, which might make you feel calm for a little while. But these feelings don't last long.

⇨ It's the same with exercise. If you exercise obsessively to lose weight, you might feel good (or less bad) for a while, but only until the next time you lose control and binge.

⇨ If you don't eat for a long time, you might get so hungry that when you do start to eat, you can't stop.

⇨ You have to work hard to keep your eating habits secret. This leaves you little time for work, study or friends.

In one study, most people with bulimia had another problem as well, such as anxiety, mood swings, and drug or alcohol problems

---

Bulimia is a real illness, not a phase or a fad. It belongs to a group of illnesses called eating disorders. Bulimia can seriously damage your health. Also, if you have it you are more likely to get depressed than other people, and you are more likely to drink alcohol heavily. In one study, most people with bulimia had another problem as well, such as anxiety, mood swings, and drug or alcohol problems. A person with bulimia is terrified of being fat, even when their weight is normal.

It's not easy to tell if someone has bulimia. People with the disease tend to be a normal weight or near to a normal weight.

Why me?

We're not sure what causes bulimia or any eating disorder. We have some ideas, but no proof yet for any of them. Below is a list of some things that seem to go along with bulimia. We think that when someone gets bulimia, it's probably because of a combination of these things:

⇨ Fear of being fat;

⇨ Body image;

⇨ Western culture;

⇨ Emotional problems;

⇨ An imbalance of chemicals in the brain;

⇨ Genes and family history.

We know that some people are more likely to get bulimia than others. Doctors call things that make you more likely to get a certain disease risk factors.

6 August 2009

⇨ The above information is re-printed with kind permission from the British Publishing Group. Visit www.bmj.com for more information or to view references for this article.

© BMJ Publishing Group Limited ('BMJ Group') 2009

Binge eating

Information from Teens First for Health

Binge eating disorder is not as well known as anorexia nervosa and bulimia nervosa but still affects lots of people. Binge eating is when a person eats large amounts of food in one go, and feels out of control and unable to stop. It can be a symptom of the other eating disorders such as bulimia nervosa or anorexia nervosa. The difference is that people with binge eating disorder do not vomit or use laxatives or starve themselves in between binges to compensate for the extra food they have eaten, and so are very likely to gain weight.

What causes binge eating disorder and who can get it?

As with other eating disorders there is no single cause of binge eating disorder and it can affect anyone, although it is more likely to affect girls and women.

Most experts believe that it takes a combination of things to develop an eating disorder such as binge eating. Your genes, emotions, and behaviours, such as eating patterns that you learn whilst you are growing up, can all play a part.

Binge eating is very closely related to your emotions and how you are feeling. People that binge eat often suffer from depression too and use food to comfort themselves when they are feeling down or unhappy.

It is believed that some people may be more prone to overeating for biological reasons. The part of the brain that controls their appetite (the hypothalamus) and what they eat may fail to send proper messages about hunger and fullness. These ideas are still being investigated.

What are the signs and symptoms of binge eating disorder?

It's perfectly normal to overeat from time to time, most people do. And especially when you are still growing it's perfectly natural to go through phases where you feel like eating more.

But binge eating is different from normal appetite increases or overeating from time to time. People with a binge eating problem eat unusually large amounts of food on a regular basis.

There are many characteristics of a binge eating session, such as eating an unusually large amount of food (for example, a whole packet of biscuits AND half a loaf of bread), eating the food quicker than usual, eating secretly in places where no-one is around, feeling full up but not stopping eating, eating foods that are seen as naughty such as chocolate and biscuits and feeling you cannot control your eating.

After an episode of binge eating you may wish you hadn't done it and feel very guilty. It may make you upset and feel bad about yourself. You may even feel embarrassed and ashamed about your eating and feel you can't talk about it.

Because people that binge eat overeat regularly they are usually overweight or obese but people of a healthy weight can also be affected.

How is binge eating disorder normally diagnosed and treated?

Many people with binge eating problems find it hard to reach out for help because they feel embarrassed about their over-eating. So seeing you have a problem and getting to a point where you're asking – 'What can I do to help myself? – is the first step to getting better.

You may prefer to get help on your own, but it can be easier and quicker to get better if you have the support of your family, in which case the whole family would be involved in treatment. You will probably be referred to see a counsellor or therapist who will be able to talk to you about how you are feeling and why you binge eat, and help you find ways of trying to stop. You will also probably be referred to see a dietician (nutrition expert) who will help you learn about the importance of eating regularly, healthy eating, portion sizes, metabolism (how your body turns food into energy), and exercise.

There are also self-help programmes and books aimed at helping people stop binge eating.

Together your doctors, psychologist or counsellor, and dietician can help you to get over an eating disorder. They will put together an eating and exercise plan for you to help you to eat healthily and to feel better about yourself and your body. Between them they help you to manage your eating, weight and feelings.

What's going to help?

Sometimes it is hard to know what weight you should be. Have a look at our BMI (Body Mass Index) counter to find your ideal weight.

Opening up to someone can also really help, it's important to find someone who you can trust to talk to about your feelings. This may be a friend, your mum, your brother or sister or even a counsellor.

Finding a way to express your feelings, such as through music, art, dance or writing, can sometimes help you to deal with difficult emotions in a healthy way.

Looking forward

There is no quick fix for binge eating disorder. Treatment can take a long time, months or longer while you learn a healthier approach to food. But if you want to get over it, with the right help and support you can have a healthier, happier life.

For more help and information

⇨ Visit Anorexia & Bulimia Care or call their helpline on 01934 710336.
⇨ The charity beat (formerly the Eating Disorders Association) have loads of resources. You can call the adult helpline on 0845 634 1414 or the youth helpline on 0845 634 7650. The charity has also developed a booklet for young people on understanding recovery and taking steps towards it.
⇨ Young Minds provides information and advice on child mental health issues. You can ring on 0800 018 2138.

Last reviewed by Great Ormond Street Hospital: 5 August 2008

⇨ This article has been reproduced with kind permission from Children First for Health – Great Ormond Street Hospital's leading health information website for young people of all ages and parents. www.childrenfirst.nhs.uk

© Great Ormond Street Hospital 2009

Other eating disorders

Information from the Institute of Psychiatry

Binge-eating disorder

People with binge-eating disorder regularly consume large amounts of food and feel they have no control over their eating. They eat until they feel uncomfortably full and when they are not physically hungry. They eat more rapidly than normal, often alone because they are embarrassed by how much they are consuming, and feel disgusted, depressed or guilty after food. Unlike people who have bulimia, they do not attempt to compensate by purging. They are often above average in weight, have low self-esteem and feel terrible shame not only about their behaviour, but about the effect it is having on their weight (real or imagined).

Body Dysmorphic Disorder (BDD)

People with BDD are preoccupied or obsessed with defects in their appearance, either real or imagined. The obsession can focus on any part of the body, but the most common are on the face or head, specifically the skin, hair and nose. People with BDD often have low self-esteem and fear of rejection due to their perceived ugliness. While some realise that their perception is distorted, they cannot control the impulse to think about it. They often practise compulsive rituals to hide, cover or improve what they consider to be a defect. They may ask doctors to treat them with medication or carry out plastic surgery. Some even attempt their own surgery.

There are two types of BDD: non-delusional and delusional. The latter is when a person has hallucinations of a completely imagined defect, or grossly exaggerates a small defect. This is less common but more severe, and causes clinically significant distress and social impairment.

Compulsive over-eating

People with this eating disorder eat according to emotional cues rather than the physiological cues of hunger and satisfaction. Everyone 'comfort eats' from time to time, but compulsive over-eaters do this consistently as a way of filling a void they feel inside, stuffing down emotional problems and coping with daily stresses. They tend to be, but are not always, overweight, and feel terrible shame about their behaviour and also the real or imagined effect it has on their body size. Overeaters Anonymous helps people who want to stop eating compulsively.

Compulsive exercising

This involves regular bouts of intense exercise beyond what is considered safe, with the main goal being to burn calories after eating, or to give the individual permission to eat afterwards. People with this disorder feel tremendously guilty when they cannot exercise and never exercise for fun. The exercise gives an individual a feeling of power, control and/or self-respect. It is another way of avoiding emotional issues and relieving guilt and stress. Compulsive exercising is associated with a number of physical risks, including dehydration, stress fractures, osteoporosis, degenerative arthritis, amenorrhoea and reproductive problems and heart problems.

Some athletes and dancers undertake compulsive exercise and adopt disordered eating patterns – use of laxatives and diuretics, for example – to prepare for competition, but do not display the psychological symptoms of an eating disorder.

Eating Disorder Not Otherwise Specified (ED-NOS)

Individuals with disordered eating patterns who do not meet some of the essential diagnostic criteria for specific disorders like anorexia and bulimia may be diagnosed with ED-NOS. This can mean a variety of things: it may be that they have symptoms of anorexia but still menstruate, or maintain a weight within the normal range; that they purge but do not binge eat; that they have symptoms of bulimia but binge eat less than twice a week. Alternatively, they might have a mixture of anorexic and some bulimic behaviour.

Night Eating Syndrome

This has recently been recognised as a possible new form of eating disorder. It involves eating the majority of food late at night, or when waking from sleep. Often people with this problem skip eating at the beginning of the day.

Pica

This is compulsive craving for eating, chewing or licking items that have no nutritional value – chalk, plaster, paint, baking soda, starch, glue, rust, coffee grounds and cigarette ashes, for example. This phenomenon is sometimes linked to certain mineral deficiencies (like iron or zinc) and it is possibly associated with certain psychological disturbances and social deprivation.

Pica is fairly common in pregnant women and symptoms usually disappear after birth. Children with learning disabilities sometimes have pica. Complications can include lead poisoning, malnutrition, abdominal problems, intestinal obstruction, hypokalemia, hyperkalemia, mercury poisoning and dental injury.

Prader-Willi Syndrome

Prader-Willi Syndrome is a complex genetic disorder which is present from birth. People with Prader-Willi Syndrome have an insatiable appetite because of a defect in the hypothalamus that results in them never actually feeling full. Individuals are often overweight and may steal food, eat pet foods and spoiled items in a bid to sate themselves.

Children born with Prader-Willi Syndrome may have early feeding problems that lead to tube feeding, and often also have a degree of behavioural or mental health problems and learning disabilities.

Physical problems associated with the Syndrome are delayed motor development, abnormal growth, speech impairments, stunted sexual development, poor muscle tone, dental problems, obesity and diabetes type 2. The Prader-Willi Syndrome Association (UK) is a charitable organisation that supports people with Prader-Willi Syndrome, their families, carers, and the professionals who work with them.

Sleep Eating Disorder (SED-NOS)

People with SED-NOS binge on unusually large quantities of food, usually high in sugar or fat, while they are sleep walking. They mostly do not remember these binge-eating episodes and are at risk from unintentional self-injury while sleep walking. People with SED-NOS are often anxious, tired, stressed and angry, and tend to be overweight.

⇨ The above information is reprinted with kind permission from the Institute of Psychiatry. Visit www.iop.kcl.ac.uk for more information on this and other related topics.

© Institute of Psychiatry

Bullying and eating disorders

Information from beat

Bullying – the vicious cycle

The largest survey of its kind to date of 600 young people with eating disorders has revealed that almost half felt that bullying had contributed to their illness.

beat – the national campaigning charity supporting people affected by eating disorders – carried out the survey and has discovered that out of those surveyed 91% had experienced bullying and 46% felt it contributed to their eating disorder. Nearly half were bullied over a period of two to five years and 11% six years or more.

Chief Executive Susan Ringwood commented: 'These results show just what a traumatic effect this sort of behaviour amongst peers can have. Bullying undermines young peoples' self-confidence and lowers their self-esteem raising the risk of eating disorders. Eating disorders are complex with no single cause but bullying is a significant factor for too many people. beat is calling for urgent, detailed research into links with eating disorders – to try and help pupils walk away from bullies without any side effects.'

Case study: Sam T

'I only had one friend in high school, but even he bullied me when the others were around. A lot of my classmates didn't want to associate with me in case they got picked on too.

'As the bullying grew worse and more kids joined in, I would run out of lessons to escape the abuse. I hid in the boys' toilets where I knew I wouldn't be found. There I would comfort eat to ease the tension and anxiety that had built up inside me throughout the day and I began to make myself sick. Over time, it developed into bulimia and it took me many years to recover.'
19 November 2009

⇨ The above information is reprinted with kind permission from beat. Visit www.b-eat.co.uk for more information.

© beat

Healthy food obsession sparks rise in new disorder

Fixation with healthy eating can be sign of serious psychological disorder

Eating disorder charities are reporting a rise in the number of people suffering from a serious psychological condition characterised by an obsession with healthy eating.

The condition, orthorexia nervosa, affects equal numbers of men and women, but sufferers tend to be aged over 30, middle-class and well-educated.

The condition was named by a Californian doctor, Steven Bratman, in 1997, and is described as a 'fixation on righteous eating'. Until a few years ago, there were so few sufferers that doctors usually included them under the catch-all label of 'Ednos' – eating disorders not otherwise recognised. Now, experts say, orthorexics take up such a significant proportion of the Ednos group that they should be treated separately.

'I am definitely seeing significantly more orthorexics than just a few years ago,' said Ursula Philpot, chair of the British Dietetic Association's mental health group. 'Other eating disorders focus on quantity of food but orthorexics can be overweight or look normal. They are solely concerned with the quality of the food they put in their bodies, refining and restricting their diets according to their personal understanding of which foods are truly "pure".'

Orthorexics commonly have rigid rules around eating. Refusing to touch sugar, salt, caffeine, alcohol, wheat, gluten, yeast, soya, corn and dairy foods is just the start of their diet restrictions. Any foods that have come into contact with pesticides, herbicides or contain artificial additives are also out.

The obsession about which foods are 'good' and which are 'bad' means orthorexics can end up malnourished. Their dietary restrictions commonly cause sufferers to feel proud of their 'virtuous' behaviour even if it means

By Amelia Hill

that eating becomes so stressful their personal relationships can come under pressure and they become socially isolated.

The obsession about which foods are 'good' and which are 'bad' means orthorexics can end up malnourished

'The issues underlying orthorexia are often the same as anorexia and the two conditions can overlap but orthorexia is very definitely a distinct disorder,' said Philpot. 'Those most susceptible are middle-class, well-educated people who read about food scares in the papers, research them on the Internet, and have the time and money to source what they believe to be purer alternatives.'

Deanne Jade, founder of the National Centre for Eating Disorders, said: 'There is a fine line between people who think they are taking care of themselves by manipulating their diet and those who have orthorexia. I see people around me who have no idea they have this disorder. I see it in my practice and I see it among my friends and colleagues.'

Jade believes the condition is on the increase because 'modern society has lost its way with food'. She said: 'It's everywhere, from the people who think it's normal if their friends stop eating entire food groups, to the trainers in the gym who [promote] certain foods to enhance performance, to the proliferation of nutritionists, dieticians and naturopaths [who believe in curing problems through entirely natural methods such as sunlight and massage].

'And just look in the bookshops – all the diets that advise eating according to your blood type or metabolic rate. This is all grist for the mill to those looking for proof to confirm or encourage their anxieties around food.'

16 August 2009

© *Guardian News & Media Ltd 2009*

Do we all have disordered eating?

Our obsession with food is so far-reaching that at least one leading expert says that we all have 'food issues.' Is she right?

By Victoria Hoban

Eating disorders are not a recent phenomenon, but they have gone from being rarely mentioned, to an issue that is dominating the headlines. According to the Eating Disorders Association, two per cent of the UK population has a clinical eating disorder, yet this undersized minority has infiltrated our definition of beauty.

In 2006, when models with a body-mass index (BMI) of less than 18 were banned from Madrid Fashion Week, organisers admitted this ruled out a third of potential participants. A media frenzy ensued, with size-zero models being blamed for pressurising young women into starving themselves. At the same time, the Government tells us that obesity rates have quadrupled in the past 25 years: British children are some of the most overweight in the world.

Between these two extremes lies a more worrying trend: an acceptable, mainstream obsession with food. Cutting out dairy, wheat or carbohydrates, or striving to 'eat organic' are commonplace, fuelled by food gurus, celebrity-fad diets and health scares. Steven Bratman, a US doctor, has coined the term 'orthorexia nervosa' to define an obsession with only eating healthy foods of a certain quality. Binge-eating and 'Eating Disorder Not Otherwise Specified' (EDNOS), also known as 'sub-clinical' eating disorders, are a cause for concern.

Robin Fox, the anthropologist, describes food as a 'profoundly social urge', something we want to share and enjoy: a symbol of survival, love and security. 'Cooking,' he says, 'is a symbol of our humanity and our place in society.' Where does that leave the 72 per cent of us who microwave ready meals?

Have we lost sight of what eating is all about? Is our anxiety about obesity ruling out a relaxed attitude to food? Are we on the verge of being a nation of disordered eaters – or are we already there?

'Everybody worries about food'

Dr Dee Dawson, 59, is medical director of the Rhodes Farm Clinic in London, dedicated to the treatment of children with eating disorders. She says:

'Everybody has issues with food these days and even so-called "healthy eating" is often not healthy at all. Disordered eating can be seen in many guises: swinging from one fad to the next, constantly dieting, trying to find the "one way" that will make life easy.

'Celebrities such as Victoria Beckham may not actually have anorexia, but they are not good role models. I was looking for a magazine to take to one of my teenage anorexic patients in hospital, but there wasn't one that didn't have the word "diet" on its cover. To me, that is appalling.

'Today, everyone has an opinion on how we should eat. You couldn't take all the advice without being a slave to it. It's this all-or-nothing attitude that's the problem. The film *Super Size Me* made me really angry: if you drank pomegranate juice every day, three times a day, you would become ill. Eating burgers, pizza or chips is alright – as long as it's all in moderation.

'The issue starts with recommendations made by the Government: having said that children should only eat a certain percentage of a chocolate bar, it has now decreed a ban on advertising junk food on children's TV. It's simplistic to think this will

I don't think this is going to do our cholesterol much good!

end childhood obesity. I don't know if this is because it wants to look like something is being done. Now Jamie Oliver has turned children off school meals, too, but kids like food with fat in it – we all do.

'Everybody worries about what to eat, but in the '50s and '60s we had chips, mash, suet, full-fat milk and custard. But we weren't obese because we didn't get driven to school or play computer games all day. It's our lifestyle and lack of exercise that must change.'

'Our food obsession is a conspiracy'

Dr John Briffa specialises in nutritional and natural medicine. He works in private practice in London and gives advice via his website. He also writes a nutrition column in the *Observer Magazine*.

'It's true that our eating has become more disordered in the past few decades, but many people still have a functional relationship with food. I have a conspiracy theory that our obsession with food is hugely driven by industry. We are indoctrinated by images and messages every day: it's a form of brainwashing. The more people believe they have to lose weight, the more diet products the big companies sell.

'Most people can't afford to eat well. It isn't cheap. Have you seen the price of fish? If you were on a budget, would you shop at a farmers' market? The Government could subsidise healthy food. Instead, we get health scares and diet initiatives. The public no longer has the confidence to follow its intuition. The best foods for us are meat, fish, eggs, fruit and vegetables – not reduced-fat cereals and diet cola. Instead, we eat a low-calorie diet that doesn't satisfy us and affects our emotional state. If you play the calorie-counting game in the day, by the evening your body is screaming for something you didn't give it. We need to get back to a diet that is more primal in nature, to eating the foods that we were designed to eat.'

⇨ The above information is re-printed with kind permission from *Psychologies*. Visit www.psychologies. co.uk for more information.

© *Psychologies*

The rise of male eating disorders

Eating disorders among men are on the rise, with recent NHS findings showing that as many as a quarter of people who suffer from eating disorders are male

The NHS Information Centre (NHS IC) research – *The Adult Psychiatric Morbidity Survey 2007* – published last month, surveyed 7,461 people in England over 16. It found that an alarming 6.4 per cent of adults had a problem with food, a figure much higher than previously thought.

Females are ten times more likely than males to suffer from anorexia or bulimia, according to the Royal College of Psychiatrists. However, the NHS research suggests that eating disorders are becoming more common in boys and men.

Eating disorders in men can take different forms to those in women, as they 'tend to be more focused on body image', Mary George from eating disorder charity beat said. She explained that 'visits to the gym become obsessive as does the desire to change body shape – this then becomes accompanied by controlling calorie intake which leads to a full-blown eating disorder'.

Common disorders

The most common forms of eating disorder are anorexia nervosa, where individuals starve themselves and excessively exercise to lose weight, and bulimia, in which they binge on food and then purge through vomiting or laxative use. Anorexia accounts for around one in ten cases in adults, according to figures from the National Institute for Health and Clinical Excellence (NICE), whereas bulimia accounts for a third of all cases, with other disorders such as compulsive eating making up the rest.

The disorders can range in severity and can be a major cause of serious psychological distress. The physical impact of a disorder such as anorexia can be devastating, resulting in drastic weight loss, low mood, a loss of periods in women, and in more acute cases, heart problems and osteoporosis.

In its eating disorder guidelines, NICE states that some studies have identified eating disorders as having the highest mortality rate of all mental disorders, illustrating the potential severity of these disorders.

A taboo subject

'Many men don't realise that they have an eating disorder and are reluctant to seek help when they do feel they have a problem,' commented beat's Mary George on why eating disorders are usually associated with women.

The silence surrounding male anorexia and bulimia has meant the issue has become something of a taboo subject, but it was cast under the spotlight last year when former deputy prime minister, John Prescott, admitted that he had suffered from bulimia in the past.

Following Mr Prescott's revelation, Ms George said the charity's helplines 'had ten times the normal number of calls for men who hadn't realised they had an eating disorder until then'.

The authors of the NHS survey concluded that although research into male eating disorders was expanding, 'men with eating disorders are a group that have been neglected in research, policy and clinical practice in this area'.

A complex issue – for both sexes

Problems with food can begin when it is used to cope with those times when someone is bored, anxious, angry, lonely, ashamed or sad, or when it is used as a crutch to help relieve painful situations, says beat.

The recent tragic death of 18-year-old Alice Rae refocuses from beyond the statistics the very real and human cost of anorexia. Alice died in January of this year; found dead in bed by her mother at the family home in Houghton, Hampshire, after battling with anorexia.

The fashion industry has come under recent scrutiny for its promotion of 'size zero' models and the message this gives out to young women about body image. But specialists, such as the National Centre for Eating Disorders, suggest reasons why someone should develop an eating disorder are complex, and each case is individual. Factors such as low self-esteem, family relationships, problems with friends, dealing with grief, problems at work or university, or sexual or emotional abuse can all play a part.

Help at hand?

Eating disorders are serious mental health issues and can be very distressing for both those with the disorder and their families, as studies show.

According to a report published by beat in February 2008 entitled *Failing Families?*, 79 per cent of families surveyed said that an eating disorder had caused lasting damage to their lives. Relationship breakdown, problems at work caused by the need to take time off to provide care and support, damage to friendships and social life and a negative impact on other children in the family were all listed as factors.

Despite NICE guidance advising that 'families and carers should be informed of self-help and support groups and offered the opportunity to participate in such groups', beat's survey found that only 12 per cent

of families felt they had access to the amount of support they needed and 23 per cent had no support at all.

The NHS survey reinforces this need for improved support and treatment of those with eating disorders, finding that four in five adults (81 per cent) who screened positive for an eating disorder were not receiving any counselling, medication or therapy for a mental or emotional problem.

In response to the NHS report findings, Conservative health spokesperson Anne Milton said: 'These figures are shocking. We are failing to get across to young people today the dangers they face when they abuse food. At one end of the scale we have

some frightening statistics on obesity and on the other end of the scale we have many people suffering from this tragic illness.'

For men or women who are experiencing emotional distress due to an eating or body-image problem – Samaritans offers impartial and non-judgmental support 24 hours a day by phone 08457 909090 (GB), or 1850 609090 (ROI), email jo@samaritans.org or face to face; visit www.samaritans.org to find your local branch.
25 February 2009

⇨ Information from the Samaritans. Visit www.samaritans.org for more.
© Samaritans

Size zero bad news for bones

Information from the University of Bristol

New research from the Children of the 90s project suggests that teenage girls who are too thin may be putting their bones at risk. It has long been known that the amount of muscle in the body is related to bone growth, but this new study shows that fat mass is also important in building bone, particularly in girls.

The researchers looked at over 4,000 young people aged 15, using sophisticated scanning techniques (DXA and pCQT) that calculated the shape and density of their bones, as well as how much body fat they had.

Those with higher levels of fat tended to have larger and thicker bones. This connection was particularly marked in the girls.

For example, one key measure showed that in girls, a five kilogram increase in fat mass was associated with an eight per cent increase in the circumference of the tibia (lower leg bone).

As girls tend to have higher levels of fat than boys, even when they are normal weight, these findings suggest that fat plays an important role in female bone development.

Building strong bones in youth is particularly important for women, as they are three times more likely to develop osteoporosis, and they suffer two to three times more hip fractures than men.

Jon Tobias, Professor of Rheumatology and leader of the research, said: 'There is a good deal of pressure on teenage girls to be thin, but they need to be aware that this could endanger their developing skeleton and put them at increased risk of osteoporosis.

'Many people think that exercise is the key to losing weight and building strong bones at the same time – but this may only be true up to a point. If you do a good deal of low impact exercise, such as walking, you will certainly lose fat but you may not be able to put enough stress on the bones to build them significantly. To offset the detrimental effect of fat loss on your bones, it may be important to include high impact exercise as well, such as running or jumping.'
5 January 2010

⇨ The above information is reprinted with kind permission from the University of Bristol. Visit www.bristol.ac.uk for more information.
© University of Bristol

Some facts

Information from Men Get Eating Disorders Too

Prevalence

Due to secrecy and the imperceptible nature of eating disorders, it is difficult to determine exactly how many men have the conditions at any one time. Figures range from 10–25% of eating disorders cases being male. However, many experts believe that these stats are an underestimate due to the difficulties men face in getting help. Recent research by the NHS Information Centre suggests that 6.4% (2.7 million) showed signs of some sort of eating disorder and men made up a quarter. It could be interpreted that this represents a growing trend, though at present there are no stats gathered around diagnosis and treatment.

Age of onset

Males of any age can develop an eating disorder but are most likely to begin between 14 and 25. It is not unusual to have an eating disorder in middle age.

Risk factors

Comparatively little research has been done into eating disorders among males but it does seem apparent that many of the risk factors are applicable in men. In particular the role of eating disorders being a coping mechanism, or expression of underlying emotional stress, and this is applicable to males as much as it is females, thus any unresolved distress consequently presents a risk to developing eating problems the same as in females.

In addition, there are a number of other risk factors that can contribute:
⇨ They were overweight as children and/or teased about their size.
⇨ They are dieting – one of the most powerful eating disorder triggers in both males and females, and as many as 70% of young people will diet at one time.
⇨ They participate in sport that demands a particular body build (thin or big). Runners or jockeys are at higher risk of developing anorexia and bulimia, while footballers or weight lifters will focus on getting bigger (known as 'bigorexia'). Wrestlers who try to shed pounds quickly before a match so they can compete in a lower weight category seem to be at special risk. Body builders are at risk if they deplete body fat and fluid reserves to achieve high definition.

⇨ They have a job or profession that demands thinness. Male models, actors and general entertainers seem to be at higher risk than the general population.
⇨ Some, but not all, male sufferers will be gay or bisexual. There is debate about why the gay and bisexual male community is at particular risk, but this may be partly because they are judged on attractiveness in the same way that women are in the heterosexual community. Fear of coming out and worry about rejection is also a possibility. In a study carried out by the Eating Disorder Association, they found that 20% of male sufferers were gay, representing twice the proportion of gay men in the general population.
⇨ Living in a culture with fixed diets and physical appearance is also a risk factor. Male underwear models and men on the front pages of male fitness magazines or gay interest publications lead other males to compare themselves with these so-called 'ideal' body types. So do ads for men's hair and skin care products. Weight loss and workout programmes, as well as cosmetic surgery procedures, with the goal of chiselled muscularity can lead to the same sort of body dissatisfaction that afflicts women who read fashion magazines and watch movies or TV shows featuring so-called perfect people.

Comparatively little research has been done into eating disorders among males

---

A study at the University of Florida found that young men's beliefs about the perfect body size has changed over the past two decades: this can be put down to the cultural endorsement of the 'perfect' male body (i.e. the Daniel Craig or David Beckham-style muscular look – complete with six pack, toned arms and a slim waist). Researchers found that teens were increasingly experiencing body dissatisfaction, changing eating habits and using anabolic steroids and dietary supplements to control weight and gain muscle. Worryingly, a separate study at the University of Illinois found that the influence of abnormally muscle-bound characters in kids' computer games drove boys as young as eight to try and build up their muscles.

⇨ The above information is reprinted with kind permission from Men Get Eating Disorders Too. Visit www.mengetedstoo.co.uk for more.
© *Men Get Eating Disorders Too*

Eating disorders over 40

Though anorexia is often linked with teenage girls, more women over 40 are now coming forward to be treated for this life-threatening eating disorder

By Emma Cowing

To the casual outsider, Mari's* life would have seemed normal. In her early forties, she was a single mum with a teenage daughter. She worked full-time and also helped her mother care for her sick father. She wasn't a big socialiser, but was close to her family. Had you looked closer, though, you might have seen the cracks.

She always layered her clothes, wearing several jumpers, one on top of the other. She never ate lunch in the office, claiming that she preferred to eat a big breakfast instead. She didn't go out for coffee with her colleagues, and never joined them on office nights out. When she cooked dinner for the family, she'd often remember she'd left the oven on just as she was bringing her own plate out of the kitchen, and would turn back to go and switch it off.

Still, when Mari was admitted to the Priory hospital in Glasgow suffering from anorexia nervosa and weighing little more than five stone, many of her relatives, friends and colleagues were shocked.

'I did a lot to try and hide it from people,' confesses Mari, who, now aged 46, has since had a further two spells in hospital and currently weighs seven stone. 'I was very defensive with people who wanted to talk to me about it and very secretive about my behaviour. The first time I went into hospital, someone from my workplace told me she had no idea there was anything wrong with me. Nobody in my workplace knew at all. I would always avoid situations where there was food, because I didn't want to be put in a position where I couldn't cope with it.'

Mari is one of a growing number of women over 40 who have recently come out of the shadows and admitted to struggling with an eating disorder. Anorexia and bulimia are traditionally seen as the province of teenage girls, but there is a growing understanding that they also affect older women. Although no official statistics are yet available, anecdotal evidence from doctors and clinics across the country suggests that the number of older women now being treated for eating disorders is on the increase.

'We are more and more aware of older people coming forward with eating disorders,' says Mary George, spokeswoman for beat, formerly the National Eating Disorders Association. 'For some, it might be something they've never managed to shake off entirely – they can be "professional" anorexics, if you like, who have suffered in silence since their teenage years. They manage to maintain an eating disorder and still live a fairly normal life.'

This was certainly the case for Mari, who first developed problems with her eating habits when she was 16.

'I was comfort eating and I became quite heavy. After about two years, something just clicked and I started controlling my food. Initially it was just [about] losing the extra weight, but it went from there.

'For years I was a functioning anorexic, bringing up my daughter and working full time. I was in denial for a lot of those years. For a long time I didn't know what was wrong with me. I knew something was wrong, but I felt incredibly isolated.'

'We are seeing increased numbers in the amount of older women being presented for treatment,' says Dr Alex Yellowlees, lead clinician at the eating disorders unit at the Priory hospital in Glasgow, many of whose patients are NHS referrals.

'Partly it is because, in the general population at large, there is an increased awareness of eating disorders and their nature and severity, and the fact that they don't just affect teenage girls. There is also more of an awareness among the medical profession about eating disorders. GPs and psychologists are now

identifying these patients more readily than they once did and referring them for specialist treatment.'

When Mari first saw a psychologist about her problems she was in her early thirties and there was far more ignorance surrounding the treatment of anorexia. 'I was given anti-depressants and that was really it. I just sort of went back to managing and no more.' In fact she had been prescribed Prozac, which, while lifting her mood, did little to address the underlying issues of her anorexia and can in fact act as an appetite suppressant.

> **'There is no woman in our society today who escapes the pressure that is upon her to achieve some body ideal or even the thin ideal'**

Mari reached her lowest point about three years ago, following her first stint in hospital. 'My father's health was dramatically deteriorating. I was looking after him and he eventually died. At that stage my daily diet was very bad: I might have a sachet of porridge oats with water, an Oxo cube with hot water – but I wouldn't have a whole one, I'd ration it throughout the day – and maybe a small soya dessert or pot of yoghurt. My intake was probably not much more than 500 calories a day.'

Even then she didn't understand how serious the situation was. 'I knew I could barely walk up and down stairs, but it crept up on me so gradually that it wasn't until I got to hospital again I realised there was a very strong chance that I would die. That bothered me, because the thought that my mother and my daughter would lose me to starvation was really distressing. By that point I really didn't care for my own sake, though.'

Such rock-bottom experiences seem to be common among older women battling lifelong problems with their eating. 'The situation can be that they had an eating disorder earlier on in life and something triggers it to come back,' says George. 'It can be

a divorce, a bereavement or any sort of emotional trauma.'

But as well as the number of women who have suffered from an eating disorder since their teens and are only now seeking treatment, there is also disturbing evidence that some women in their forties and fifties are developing an eating disorder for the first time.

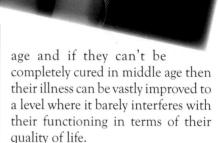

'There is a group of older women who develop anorexia or bulimia later in life, and it tends to be down to the older celebrity role models that we have now,' says George. 'I'm not suggesting that is the entire cause, but you do have the Madonnas, the Sharon Stones, these slightly older role models who have the time and the money to look incredible. It puts a lot of pressure on women who think that's what they should look like.' With television programmes bearing titles like *10 Years Younger*, plastic surgery becoming increasingly acceptable and women in their fifties expected to look as if they are still in their thirties, it is perhaps not surprising the pressure is manifesting itself.

'There is no woman in our society today who escapes the pressure that is upon her to achieve some body ideal or even the thin ideal,' says Yellowlees. 'Women are under this constant pressure to be moving to some level of bodily perfection as our society sees it.'

George believes this constant striving for perfection can have a devastating affect on some minds. 'A lot of professional women are perfectionists, and this, unfortunately, is part and parcel of how they see perfection, in a way that others wouldn't. They have unrealistic ideals.'

So what, then, is the prognosis for older women suffering from eating disorders?

'To a certain extent, the length of someone's illness can affect the outcome,' says Yellowlees. 'But at the same time, people can recover at any

age and if they can't be completely cured in middle age then their illness can be vastly improved to a level where it barely interferes with their functioning in terms of their quality of life.

'Sometimes, older women – because they're more mature – can take more personal responsibility for their recovery. Perhaps they are in a relationship, and they're in an occupation where they are functioning in society, so they take a lot more responsibility for themselves.'

For Mari, recovery has been a long road. At seven stone, she has lost weight since her last hospital visit and for now is simply trying to maintain her weight.

'It gets harder as you get older because there's more of a physical toll on your body,' she says. 'When you're younger you can function at a lower energy rate than when you're older. The way things are for me personally, I wonder if having a lifetime of this battle means it's just hardwired into my brain. I'm constantly sending negative messages to myself – it's the way my mind always works, so I wonder how I will manage ever to change that.'

She deeply regrets not having sought help at a younger age.

'I really wish I had gone to the doctor when I was 18 years old and said, "Look, I'm in really deep trouble. I literally cannot eat." I think even just saying to someone "help me" would have made a massive difference'.

* *Mari's name has been changed.*
27 April 2009

© *Scotsman*

Are you a drunkorexic?

Information from www.drinkaware.co.uk

Skipping meals in order to save calories to drink alcohol is becoming worryingly popular amongst young women. What seems like a harmless tactic to have fun and stay thin could develop into something a lot more serious.

Pasta or pinot grigio? A healthy meal or a half pint? These are the kind of questions a drunkorexic considers come Friday night. They'll normally opt for the liquid option.

A drunkorexic is someone who skips meals so they can binge drink without putting on weight

---

Readers of women's magazines will probably know about drunkorexia – a phenomenon which can be traced back to the cocktail bars of New York.

A drunkorexic is someone who skips meals so they can binge drink without putting on weight.

Calorie conscious

It mostly affects weight-conscious young women. To them, a night on the town means an evening – or a day – without a proper meal. Either that or, feeling they need to drink to fit in, they'll calculate how many calories they can consume before having a few drinks.

Although alcohol itself doesn't actually contain fat, it is packed with

drinkaware.co.uk
for the facts about alcohol

calories. With mixers (and if you drink more than your weekly recommended allowance), the calories start adding up.

While it's good to be savvy about the calories in your favourite tipple – and you can use the Drinkaware drinks calculator to do just that – don't let it become an obsession that encourages you to skip meals. Eating healthily before or during drinking is more the direction you want to be going in.

Coping strategy

'There's huge pressure on women to drink and look thin,' says Louise Noble, chief dietitian at the Berkshire Healthcare Trust. 'It means they're often missing out on important nutrition, so they can get drunk with their mates.

'In my experience, many young women will find the only way they can cope with both is to drink rather than eat, to substitute alcohol for food.'

Noble says the problem is heightened by images of celebrities 'lauded' for staying stick-thin while maintaining a hectic social schedule.

Dangerous routine

Skipping dinner so you can party like (and still have the figure of) Lindsay Lohan might sound harmless, but it could become part of your weekend routine. Last year a report published in the American journal *Biological Psychiatry* found that up to a third of bulimics struggle with alcohol or drug abuse.

Now dietitians have coined the term 'drunkorexia' because they believe, based on their work with clients, that there is a link between binge drinking and eating disorders, though further clinical investigation into this connection is needed.

Reality check

'Someone who skips a meal to drink isn't necessarily going to become an anorexic,' said Emma Healey, spokesperson for eating disorders charity beat. 'But it's obviously highly unhealthy and if people are vulnerable it could be a high-risk behaviour.'

The problem comes when someone's drunkorexia means they start obsessing over food

---

Healey says the problem comes when someone's drunkorexia means they start obsessing over food and it begins to start controlling them.

'We always groan when the media start talking about the latest "orexias". The latest one was "pregorexia" – mums-to-be who obsess over their weight. But we do come across drunkorexia in the work we do with young people, even if they don't call it that. It's a difficult and sensitive area.'

So, what seems like a harmless tactic to have fun and stay thin could develop into something a lot more serious.

Simply put, for the calorie conscious, it makes sense to cut back on alcohol rather than food.
29 September 2009

⇨ The above information is reprinted with kind permission from Drinkaware. Visit www.drinkaware.co.uk for more information.
© *Drinkaware*

Girls' attitudes

What girls think about appearance and body image

Girlguiding UK is the largest organisation for girls and young women in the United Kingdom. Around half a million girls and young women take part in our dynamic, informal learning programmes and benefit from time spent in a safe, girl-only space. For 100 years the organisation has adapted and moved with the times to remain relevant to each new generation of girls. Now, at the start of our centenary year, we have completed our largest piece of research to date. For the first time, we have broadened our scope beyond surveying our members and have instead undertaken a comprehensive study of the attitudes of girls and young women across the UK to the world around them. In doing this, we are not only providing a platform for girls' voices to be heard, but also ensuring that as a youth organisation we continue to remain relevant to the needs of girls today. Find out more about guiding today at www.girlguiding.org.uk. All the results from the Girls' Attitudes Survey can be found on a new interactive website, where you can search the results by theme, region and age group, access spreadsheets of individual datasets, as well as read in detail about the research methodology and download pdf versions of our reports: www.girlguiding.org.uk/girlsattitudes

Appearance and body image

Among the youngest girls, the majority were happy with the way they looked (82 per cent of 7- to 11-year-olds). Older girls were significantly less happy with their appearance – 64 per cent of 11- to 16-year-olds and 69 per cent of 16- to 21-year-olds. In fact, 60 per cent of the youngest girls surveyed, those aged between 7 and 9 years, said they were 'very happy' with their appearance, dropping sharply to just 27 per cent of 10- to 11-year-olds, suggesting that from the age of ten upwards girls start to judge their appearance more harshly. More than one in ten 11- to 16-year-olds said they were 'not at all happy' with their appearance (compared to only two per cent of girls aged 7 to 11 and seven per cent of those aged 16 to 21), indicating that self-esteem – high in the primary school years and starting to rise again in the later teens – appears to drop significantly during the early teenage years.

> **Even by the age of 10 to 11 years, something has changed: 79 per cent would like to change some aspect of their appearance**

A significant number of girls across the entire age range could identify at least one thing they would like to change about their appearance. 72 per cent of 7- to 11-year-olds would like to change some aspect: 14 per cent would like to alter their teeth in some way, 12 per cent their hair and ten per cent their skin/spots. However, it is clear that even by the age of 10 to 11 years, something has changed: 79 per cent would like to change some aspect of their appearance, with 12 per cent of girls wishing to make themselves thinner (compared to only five per cent of 7- to 9-year-olds). Being thinner is the most popular choice for the 11- to 16-year-olds (21 per cent) and 16- to 21-yearolds (33 per cent) and is far more of a concern than skin/spots (ten per cent of 11- to 16-year-olds; nine per cent of 16- to 21-year-olds) or body shape (14 per cent of 11- to 16-year-olds; nine per cent of 16- to 21-year-olds).

41 per cent of 11- to 16-year-olds categorically said they would not consider surgery to alter the way they looked, and a further 13 per cent were

HAPPY 10th BIRTHDAY DARLING!
DADDY WILL BE HERE IN A MINUTE...
HE'S JUST REMOVING THE MIRRORS
FROM YOUR ROOM.

unsure. However, those attending a school whose performance was rated outstanding or good were twice as likely to say no compared to those at schools rated satisfactory or poor (43 per cent compared to 19 per cent). Of those who would undergo some form of procedure, the most popular was a dental brace (cited by 21 per cent). A further 12 per cent would consider more invasive procedures, such as gastric band or cosmetic surgery, and five per cent would consider having Botox.

Among 16- to 21-year-olds the picture changes – one in two (50 per cent) would consider surgery to change their appearance. Of the options presented, the most popular was cosmetic surgery, with a quarter of girls now prepared to consider it. This figure was highest in Scotland, where 39 per cent of girls are keen, compared to just 11 per cent in Northern Ireland and 24 per cent overall. Older girls are also more likely to consider laser eye surgery (17 per cent). A similar number would consider a dental brace, and one in ten would consider weight loss surgery.

The way forward

A panel of young women aged between 15 and 24 from within the guiding movement came together to review the findings of the survey and to make their recommendations to both Girlguiding UK and other interested audiences.

What girls said...

Based both on their own experiences and the findings of the survey, girls had strong feelings on this subject. These are some of their key points.

Building up self-esteem from a young age is vital for developing a healthy approach to life. Youth organisations can play an important role by providing a safe space for girls to gain personal achievements, which in turn build up self-esteem, and schools should start focusing on self-esteem at a younger age, e.g. by introducing high-quality PSHE [Personal, Social and Health Education] provision earlier.

The pressures of modern society inevitably lead girls to pin their sense of self-worth on their appearance unless they are given other reasons to feel good about themselves. All those working with young women should be encouraged to provide opportunities for girls to achieve personally through any activity they enjoy doing. The continued focus on peer pressure as the root cause of unhealthy behaviour is actually narrowing the breadth of support available on health issues. Those people working with young people should address issues of access, which prevent young women, particularly those no longer in formal education and those living in rural areas, from getting impartial advice and support.

While the content of magazines etc has improved significantly on issues surrounding body image and self-esteem, the panel felt that free gifts of make-up items and advertising from cosmetic surgery clinics often undermine these positive messages.
Fieldwork: 11 May–15 July 2009

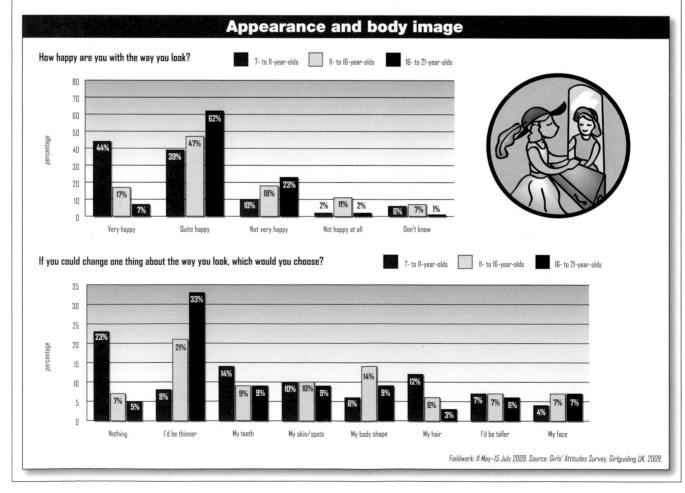

Appearance and body image

How happy are you with the way you look?

Legend: 7- to 11-year-olds | 11- to 16-year-olds | 16- to 21-year-olds

	Very happy	Quite happy	Not very happy	Not happy at all	Don't know
7- to 11-year-olds	44%	39%	10%	2%	6%
11- to 16-year-olds	17%	47%	18%	11%	7%
16- to 21-year-olds	7%	62%	23%	2%	1%

If you could change one thing about the way you look, which would you choose?

Legend: 7- to 11-year-olds | 11- to 16-year-olds | 16- to 21-year-olds

	Nothing	I'd be thinner	My teeth	My skin/spots	My body shape	My hair	I'd be taller	My face
7- to 11-year-olds	23%	8%	14%	10%	6%	12%	7%	4%
11- to 16-year-olds	7%	21%	9%	10%	14%	6%	7%	7%
16- to 21-year-olds	5%	33%	9%	9%	9%	3%	6%	7%

Fieldwork: 11 May–15 July 2009. Source: Girls' Attitudes Survey, Girlguiding UK, 2009.

Anxiety over body image

National survey reveals public anxiety over body image

An unprecedented survey of people's attitudes towards body image has revealed that 90% of adults in the UK believe we care too much about the way we look, and not enough about how healthy we are.

Almost a quarter of the adult population feel depressed at some point about their body shape, and 90% believe advertisers should be using differing body sizes in their campaigns.

Research commissioned by Central YMCA, the UK's leading activity-for-health charity, has also revealed that:

⇨ 88% of people believe children to be under more pressure about their physical appearance than they were 20 years ago;

⇨ 81% of people think that pupils in secondary schools should be given an opportunity to discuss body image issues in schools

⇨ More than 50% of adults think body image issues should be addressed at a younger age (i.e. in primary school);

⇨ 77% of people believe that airbrushed photographs should carry a warning.

The 'Healthy Attitudes to Healthy Bodies' survey launches Central YMCA's campaign to raise awareness about the extent of society's obsession with body image ideals, and its associated negative impact upon the wellbeing of children, young people and adults.

'This survey illustrates a deep public unease about the growing focus on body image ideals, and we are particularly concerned about the relationship this has with the self-esteem and confidence of many in society, particularly children and young people.

'The YMCA's work with children and young people would suggest that there is an appetite for, and an urgent need to provide, a safe space and supportive environment for children and young people to debate these issues,' says Rosi Prescott, Central YMCA's CEO.

Central YMCA is calling for a debate about the use of airbrushing, including the proposed use of labelling for airbrushed images. In addition, they are campaigning for resources to be made available to help children and young people discuss body image, including having school lessons on body confidence and positive body image within the school curricula.

Several YMCAs already work with young people to address body image concerns:

Central YMCA's Y Touring Theatre Company ran a series of workshops in primary and secondary schools across London and found that both teachers and young people felt the workshops provided a safe space for young people to explore issues surrounding body image.

Nigel Townsend, Executive Director of the Theatre Company, said: 'The workshops that we carried out in schools used a mix of electronic voting and mobile phone videos to capture what young people/children's awareness and concerns were. The results mirrored the concerns of the adults, and demonstrated how early the impact of the visual media is beginning to affect children's awareness of body image and impact on their sense of wellbeing and self-confidence.'

The workshops, entitled 'Speak Out on Bodies', were researched and developed as a teacher resource designed to support the achievement of attainment targets outlined in Key Stages 3-4 in Science, English, Drama, PE, RS, Citizenship and PSHE. They also aim to develop Emotional Intelligence working with cross curricular dimensions to address Social and Emotional Aspects of Learning (SEAL) and achieve Personal Learning and Thinking Skills (PLTS). The project will be supported by online teacher and student resources.

Some comments from young people who took part included:

'Real talk, media frenzied young girls with size 0 catwalk models have the worst idea of beauty. Juicy curves beat skinny bones any day as 9/10 guys will tell u.' Anonymous male

Bridgwater YMCA runs regular group sessions with young people to debate and discuss body image issues. One of the participants, Tash Allen, aged 18, said:

'When I was at school we didn't look at body image at all. I think it

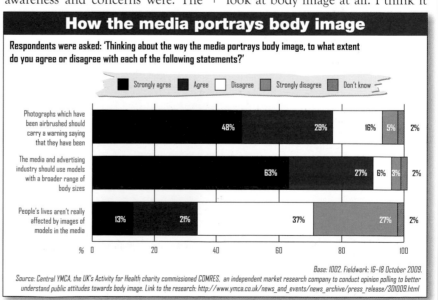

How the media portrays body image

Respondents were asked: 'Thinking about the way the media portrays body image, to what extent do you agree or disagree with each of the following statements?'

Legend: ■ Strongly agree ■ Agree □ Disagree ▨ Strongly disagree ▨ Don't know

Statement	Strongly agree + Agree	Disagree	Strongly disagree	Don't know
Photographs which have been airbrushed should carry a warning saying that they have been	48%	29%	16%	5% / 2%
The media and advertising industry should use models with a broader range of body sizes	63%	27%	6%	3% / 2%
People's lives aren't really affected by images of models in the media	13% / 21%	37%	27%	2%

% 0   20   40   60   80   100

Base: 1002. Fieldwork: 16–18 October 2009.

Source: Central YMCA, the UK's Activity for Health charity commissioned COMRES, an independent market research company to conduct opinion polling to better understand public attitudes towards body image. Link to the research: http://www.ymca.co.uk/news_and_events/news_archive/press_release/301009.html

would have been good to do it at school but to have someone, not a teacher, to come in and talk about it. You would open up more to someone you don't know. When I moved to the YMCA I always thought about what I looked like and first impressions of other residents wasn't good, until they got to know me. I still always think about what I look like but in a more positive way.'

'The debate about body image ideals is gathering momentum and it won't go away,' says Ms Prescott.

'Germany's top woman's magazine *Brigitte* has announced that it will no longer use professional models and will instead use everyday women as models. In France, proposals have been mooted in Parliament to label airbrushed images. And in the UK, the Liberal Democrats are calling for an outright ban on airbrushing targeting under-16-year-olds.'

These views are shared by a number of other organisations. For example, Andrew McCulloch, Chief Executive of the Mental Health Foundation, said:

'Modern society puts both adults and children under enormous pressure to look a certain way and consequently many people feel inadequate and unhappy with how they look. Body image issues can lead to low self-esteem and even emotional and mental health problems.'
30 October 2009
⇨ Information from Central YMCA. Visit www.ymca.co.uk for more.
© *Central YMCA*

'Speak Out on Bodies' workshops from the YMCA
'Speak Out on Bodies' is a two-hour workshop with integrated debate for a maximum of 40 students per workshop, and Y Touring are planning future workshops with schools to debate and discuss body image issues. If your school would like to run a 'Speak Out on Bodies' workshop, or for further information, please email info@ytouring.org.uk or call Y Touring on 020 7520 3090.

The workshops were researched and developed as a teacher resource designed to support the achievement of attainment targets outlined in Key Stages 3–4 in Science, English, Drama, PE, RS, Citizenship and PSHE. They also aim to develop Emotional Intelligence, working with cross curricular dimensions to address Social and Emotional Aspects of Learning (SEAL) and achieve Personal Learning and Thinking Skills (PLTS). The project will be supported by online teacher and student resources.

Girls 'damaged' by mum's diet

Girls whose mothers are on a diet are almost twice as likely to have an eating disorder, a poll of more than 500 teenagers found today

Many girls say their mother has the biggest influence on their own self-image and they feel damaged by the effects of their mum's dieting and views on food.

The survey of 512 teenage girls, with an average age of 14 (age range of 12 to 18) found 6% had an eating disorder, rising to one in ten among those whose mothers diet.

Almost four out of ten girls (38%) said their mother had the biggest influence on how they perceived themselves.

Two-thirds (66%) said they had heard their mum complaining about her own weight and 56% have mothers who are on a diet.

This is despite 68% describing their mother's body size as perfectly normal.

Other findings in the survey include:
⇨ More than half of teenage girls surveyed (51%) have dieted. This becomes 59% among girls whose mothers diet.

By Jane Kirby

⇨ Almost eight out of ten (78%) girls worry about their weight – 20% say they worry about their looks all the time.
⇨ One in five girls said they are criticised by family members for being 'too big' and 51% of those

have been hurt by their parents talking about their size.
⇨ Almost one in three have been called names like 'elephant' or 'beast' by their relatives.
⇨ Among girls who get comments about their weight from their families, 58% worry about their looks all the time.
⇨ 9% of teenage girls say they are

'constantly' on a diet. Among girls whose families comment on their weight, this rose to 24%.

The survey was carried out among readers of teen magazine, *Sugar*.

Its editor Annabel Brog said girls were heavily influenced by their family's views on diet and food – so-called 'thinheritance'.

She said: 'Every single issue of *Sugar* magazine features fashion modelled by "regular" girls, with different body sizes and shapes, to prove all bodies are gorgeous when they're well fed and exercised.

'But it stands to reason that a girl's "thinheritance" – the attitude to food and body-shape she is exposed to day after day in her home – is going to be more powerful than anything we can print in a magazine.

'And of course many girls feel their mums, who typically diet and worry about their own weight, are their greatest influence.'

Psychologist Amanda Hills said: 'Children learn how to behave by watching their parents.

'Food becomes an issue when mum isn't sitting down to dinner with everyone else or is off preparing a separate meal for herself.

'And a dieting parent will label certain foods as "bad" or "wrong", which can lead to an unhealthy approach to food.

'The "drip-drip" effect of constant self-criticism in front of easily influenced teens teaches them to do likewise.

'If mum's calling herself fat, it won't be long before her daughter is too.

'I would say at least half of the people I see with an eating disorder admit that there are problems with eating in the family.'

Sugar reader Jessica, 16, from Berkshire, said: 'My mum's often saying how ugly she thinks she is in front of me.

'She wouldn't come out to dinner with us when we were on holiday last year because none of her clothes flattered her.

'I hate it – she's so beautiful and not fat at all.

'I know she doesn't mean it, but sometimes I do think it has an effect on me and might be part of why I'm so self-conscious about my weight and

chunky legs.'

Sophie, 14, from London, said: 'Dad calls me a "heifer" when I eat everything on my plate at dinner.

'The first time he said it, I was embarrassed, but told myself he was just trying to be funny.

'But he keeps saying it and I've started to think maybe I am a heifer.

'I'd never really looked at myself as "fat" or "thin" before, but I've stopped eating as much because I can't bear it any more.'

Jo, 17, from Norfolk, said: 'I was diagnosed with anorexia last year and am only just starting to eat properly again.

'Mum blames herself because she was bulimic several years ago, and she constantly talked about her fear of being fat.

'It meant that I saw food as something to be scared of and started to avoid it.'

28 October 2009

© *Press Association*

'Crisis in masculinity' leads to eating disorders

Young heterosexual men are falling prey to eating disorders such as anorexia and bulimia just as much as women and gay men – and their numbers are increasing

Dr John Morgan, a consultant psychiatrist and director of the Yorkshire Centre for Eating Disorders in Leeds, told the Annual Meeting of the Royal College of Psychiatrists in Liverpool that growing numbers of young men are increasingly dissatisfied with their bodies. In addition, the gap in the numbers of gay and straight men with eating disorders is closing.

Dr Morgan told Annual Meeting delegates that men are:
⇨ less likely to recognise their eating disorder;
⇨ more likely to be mis-diagnosed with other mental health problems such as depression and schizophrenia;
⇨ less likely to be given treatment;
⇨ less likely to be referred to a special eating disorder clinic.

Many men struggle to be referred to a specialist eating disorder clinic in the first instance. Furthermore, once they undergo treatment, many report being stigmatised as the only man in the clinic.

He said: 'By the time they go for treatment, the disorder is much further down the line. Sometimes when men overcome their reluctance, their GP is likely to say that men don't get eating disorders. So it's not just their reluctance – it's the system putting up barriers.'

Images of skeletal models or men with 'six-packs', plus a plethora of choices now open to men, is at the root of body dissatisfaction, Dr Morgan said.

'To be a young man in our society is a difficult thing. What you do and who you are is less straightforward. Women were challenged decades ago to consider which of the many different social roles they adopted. Now men are having to respond to the choices that society gives them.

'Suddenly younger straight men have similar pressures to gay men and women. There is a crisis of masculinity in our society. They are given all these roles and to simply decide to manipulate your body is a nice easy solution to all the complexities of life.'

Dr Morgan's research, drawn from a range of studies, has been accepted by the *European Eating Disorders Review*.

5 June 2009

⇨ The above information is reprinted with kind permission from the Royal College of Psychiatrists. Visit www.rcpsych.ac.uk for more.

© *Royal College of Psychiatrists*

Living on one meal a day

Teens risk health to copy stick-thin celebrities

Teenage girls are routinely missing two meals a day because they believe they need to lose weight, a major survey of children's lifestyles has revealed.

26 per cent of 14- and 15-year-olds often don't eat breakfast, 22 per cent skip lunch and ten per cent regularly go without either, the study found.

A majority of teenage girls – and 40 per cent of ten- and 11-year-olds – believed they needed to slim but few were actually overweight.

The findings will fuel concerns that the prevalence of 'size zero' models and super-slim celebrities such as Victoria Beckham is fuelling girls' obsession with their weight.

Experts warned that erratic meal patterns at such a young age could lead to girls developing eating disorders such as anorexia, bulimia or compulsive eating as well as health problems associated with them as the body is deprived of nutrients.

The survey, conducted among 32,000 ten- to 15-year-olds by the Exeter-based Schools Health Education Unit, presents a snapshot of British schoolchildren's lifestyles.

Asked about their breakfast on the

By Laura Clark and Steve Doughty

day of the poll, 26 per cent of girls aged 14 and 15 admitted eating nothing.

20 per cent of 12- and 13-year-old girls had skipped it while seven per cent of ten- and 11-year-olds had also gone without.

22 per cent of older girls and 14 per cent of 12- and 13-year-olds had skipped lunch. One in ten of the older girls had eaten neither breakfast nor lunch.

But only around ten per cent of 14- and 15-year- old girls in the study were overweight or obese.

'Most of those wanting to lose weight are within the limits of "healthy" weight, and some are already underweight,' the report said.

Figures dating back to 1991 showed an 'increasing trend of desire for weight loss', it added.

58 per cent of 14- and 15-year-old girls wanted to lose weight, as did 52 per cent of 12- and 13-year-olds. One per cent of the older girls – around 3,000 – were using laxatives.

Growing numbers of youngsters at primary school are also worried about their size and appearance, the research found.

Mary George, spokesman for beat, the eating disorders charity, warned: 'It is very unwise to skip meals in this way, especially at an age where the body is still developing and requires food for energy.

'Taken to extremes this behaviour could possibly lead the way towards an eating disorder which can destroy lives. A healthy diet and sensible exercise is vital.'

She added: 'We're all subjected daily to portrayals of unrealistic body images and these can be particularly influential on young and vulnerable young people.'

Despite a tendency to skip meals, pupils' diets are becoming healthier, the research suggests.

Consumption of chips and crisps has declined sharply over the past 20 years, although only around one in five teenagers is consuming the Government's recommended five portions of fruit and vegetables a day.

Drug-taking among schoolchildren has returned to the record levels last seen a decade and a half ago, the survey found.

18 per cent of boys aged 14 and 15 and 17 per cent of girls said they had tried cannabis. Three per cent of boys and two per cent of girls of the same age said they had tried cocaine.

The findings undermine Government claims that drug use is at a 'historic low'.

Earlier studies showed a drop in drug experimentation among 14- and 15-year-old pupils between 1996 and 1999.

But the report said: 'From 1999 onwards we have seen a recovery to about the same levels as the peak in 1995/96.'

This article first appeared in the Daily Mail, 13 October 2009.

© Associated Newspapers Ltd 2010

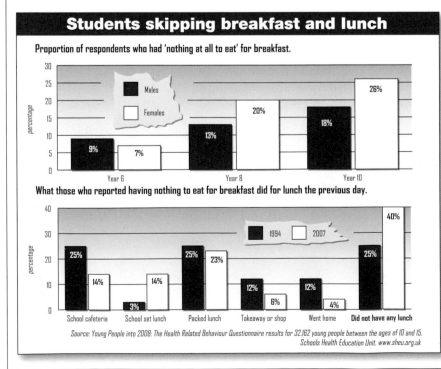

Students skipping breakfast and lunch

Proportion of respondents who had 'nothing at all to eat' for breakfast.

Males / Females

	Year 6	Year 8	Year 10
Males	9%	13%	18%
Females	7%	20%	26%

What those who reported having nothing to eat for breakfast did for lunch the previous day.

1994 / 2007

	School cafeteria	School set lunch	Packed lunch	Takeaway or shop	Went home	Did not have any lunch
1994	25%	3%	25%	12%	12%	25%
2007	14%	14%	23%	6%	4%	40%

Source: Young People into 2008: The Health Related Behaviour Questionnaire results for 32,162 young people between the ages of 10 and 15. Schools Health Education Unit. www.sheu.org.uk

Airbrushed ads damaging a generation of young women

A University of Sussex psychologist is the lead author of a report sent to UK advertising authorities condemning the use of ultra-thin, digitally altered women in adverts

Dr Helga Dittmar collaborated with experts in the field of body image to produce the paper that details scientific evidence on how the use of airbrushing to promote body perfect ideals in advertising is causing a host of problems in young women. These include eating disorders, depression, extreme exercising and encouraging cosmetic surgery.

The report, signed by 44 leading academics, doctors and clinical psychologists from the UK, USA, Australia, Brazil, Spain and Ireland, was submitted to the Committee for Advertising Practice on 9 November 2009 as part of a campaign co-ordinated by the Liberal Democrat Party, headed by Jo Swinson MP.

Dr Dittmar says: 'It is clear that most fashion advertising uses airbrushing technology, capable of changing all aspects of appearance and body shape – for example, different size eyes, thinner legs, slimmer waists and enlarged breasts. More than 100 scientific studies show that exposure to unrealistic body-perfect ideals like this in the media leads to body dissatisfaction, negative thoughts and feeling about the body, for the great majority of girls and women.'

She says the evidence suggests that adolescents are more vulnerable than adults and that young children also show negative effects on body image. 'We want to make sure that girls are educated about the unrealistic media ideals as part of the school curriculum and be sure that policy changes are used to curb the use of artificial and unhealthy body-perfect ideals in the media, particularly in under-16s.'

Commenting, Liberal Democrat MP Jo Swinson said: 'This paper spells out the real damage irresponsible airbrushing is doing to young women's physical and mental health.

'Airbrushing means that women and young girls are being bombarded with images of people with perfect skin, perfect hair and perfect figures, which are impossible to live up to. The Advertising Standards Agency received five complaints about airbrushed images last year. This year thanks to our campaign it has had almost 1,000. It now has all the scientific evidence it needs to act.

'Liberal Democrats believe in the freedom of companies to advertise but we also believe in the freedom of young people to develop their self-esteem and to be comfortable with their bodies. They shouldn't constantly feel the need to measure up to unattainable images that no-one can live up to in real life.'
10 November 2009

⇨ The above information is reprinted with kind permission from the University of Sussex. Visit www. sussex.ac.uk for more information.
© University of Sussex

Size zero: an undernourished argument

By Melissa Kite

Vogue editor Alexandra Shulman has reignited public concern over 'size zero' models by writing to the main fashion houses demanding they send magazines bigger clothes. She says the samples they provide for photoshoots are tailored for the painfully thin and she complains that this makes for disturbing pictures.

This much I agree with. What I cannot get my head around is the notion that size zero models are fuelling an epidemic in anorexia in the wider population. Look out of your window right now and the chances are that the next young woman you see is not desperately thin but podgy and out of condition. She probably has 'stomach cleavage' hanging over the top of her low rise jeans.

The fact is that in 1951 the average woman was 136lbs with a 27-inch waist and now she is 143lb with a 34-inch waist. Yes, six per cent of women are underweight, but a much more worrying 44 per cent of women are overweight.

So why do we fixate about the problem of excessive thinness? Because, I suspect, we underestimate anorexia, a serious disease and mental disorder which, like addiction, cannot be contracted simply by looking at the wrong images. Banning size zero models may or may not be a noble endeavour. But we should not kid ourselves that it will cure obsessive dieters. If they want to fixate upon an image of starvation they will find one. What is needed is better treatment.
13 June 2009

© Telegraph Media Group Limited (2009)

The fashion industry

Information from the Binge Eating Disorder Association

In the past few weeks, fashion industry professionals have been challenging ultra-thin images of beauty. Among them are London knitwear designer Mark Fast, who chose size 12 and 14 models to showcase his form-fitting dresses at London's Fashion Week show, and senior booker for Verbmodels Matan Uziel, whose company has adopted a new global guideline prohibiting use of models or actors who are either excessively slim or promote 'unhealthy' slimness. In addition, *Brigitte*, a top-selling women's fashion magazine in Germany, barred professional models from its pages in favour of 'real women'. In response to which clothing designer Karl Lagerfeld commented, 'Nobody wants to see a round woman.' During the same time period, Ralph Lauren fired model Filipa Hamilton for being 'too fat', even though her weight was in the anorexic range.

Brigitte, a top-selling women's fashion magazine in Germany, barred professional models from its pages in favour of 'real women'

BEDA advocates for individuals with all eating disorders, from those who are underweight to those who are overweight.

'We see the shame, distress, depression, anxiety and pain that result from eating disorders,' states Chevese Turner, BEDA chief executive officer. 'Individuals and our society at large are affected, and we believe it is vitally important for fashion industry leaders to commit to promoting healthier images of women and men enjoying fashion and a broader definition of beauty. While we appreciate the fashion industry's talent, we must also realise that it has a tremendous influence on our culture. We must understand that including realistic shapes and sizes helps counter the body dissatisfaction, illness, and even death that is a reality for those who are predisposed to and struggling with eating disorders. We must protest the messages based on body size and shape that undermine the self worth of girls and women and boys and men worldwide.

'On behalf of BEDA and the Academy for Eating Disorders, I congratulate the courageous fashion industry professionals who challenge the belief that the only way to be beautiful is to be thin,' Turner continues. 'BEDA urges people around the world to support those who dare to defy the unhealthy standard of "rail-thin" beauty; we encourage you to use your purchasing power and your voice to make change happen and save lives.'

Binge Eating Disorder Association (BEDA) is a national organisation focusing on the need to increase prevention, diagnosis and treatment for binge-eating disorder. Through education, outreach and support, and resources, BEDA is committed to facilitating awareness, quality of care and recovery for those who live and those who work with binge eating disorder. For more information, visit www.bedaonline.com

22 October 2009

⇨ The above information is reprinted with kind permission from the Binge Eating Disorder Association. Visit www.bedaonline.com for more.

© Binge Eating Disorder Association

Moss criticised for 'pro-anorexia comment'

By Lewis Bazley

Supermodel Kate Moss has been condemned for seeming to endorse a slogan which encourages anorexics to avoid eating.

The 35-year-old told fashion website WWD that one of her mottos is: 'Nothing tastes as good as skinny feels.'

The phrase is regularly used by anorexia and bulimia sufferers on websites endorsing the eating disorders.

In the interview Moss added: 'That's one of them. You try and remember, but it never works.'

Her remarks have been labelled 'dangerous' and 'very unhelpful' by eating disorder charity beat while Dr Carol Cooper told Sky News Online the model's comments were 'absolutely appalling'.

Katie Green, a former Ultimo lingerie model who earlier this year launched the 'Say No to Size Zero' campaign, labelled Moss' comments 'irresponsible'.

'I think Kate Moss should really have thought before she spoke like most of us do before giving interviews. Kate is a mother herself and how would parents with children suffering from eating disorders feel reading something like this?' she told the BBC.

'We are trying to get the Government to put something in place to stamp out size zero models and comments like this aren't doing anything to help that.'

19 November 2009

© Adfero

Psychiatrists urge action to tackle 'pro-ana' websites

Information from the Royal College of Psychiatrists

Psychiatrists today call for urgent action to protect vulnerable young people from the harmful influence of pro-eating disorder websites.

Even for healthy young women, viewing such websites induces low mood, low self-esteem and increased body dissatisfaction

---

So-called 'pro-ana' (pro-anorexia) and 'pro-mia' (pro-bulimia) websites have existed since the development of the Internet – but their number has soared in recent years with the growth of social networking.

Now the Royal College of Psychiatrists says the Government must do more to address the dangers of pro-eating disorder websites and keep young people safe online.

In September 2008, the Government established the UK Council for Child Internet Safety to deliver recommendations made by Professor Tanya Byron in her report *Safer Children in a Digital World*.

But members of the Royal College of Psychiatrists' Eating Disorders Section claim the Council's plans for action do not go far enough because they fail to specifically address pro-eating disorder websites. In a new position paper published today (18 September 2009), the Royal College of Psychiatrists calls on the Council to:

⇨ Expand its definition of harmful web content to include pro-eating disorder websites.

⇨ Extend its plans to moderate Internet sites that promote harmful behaviour to include pro-eating disorder websites.

⇨ Specifically address pro-eating disorder websites in its plans to raise awareness of e-safety among parents and teachers.

Professor Schmidt, chair of the Royal College of Psychiatrists' Eating Disorders Section, said: 'Pro-ana and pro-mia websites advocate anorexia nervosa or bulimia nervosa as a lifestyle choice, rather than as serious mental disorders. Research shows that, even for healthy young women, viewing such websites induces low mood, low self-esteem and increased body dissatisfaction.

'The broader societal context in which pro-ana and pro-mia sites thrive is one where young women are constantly bombarded with toxic images of supposed female perfection that are impossible to achieve, make women feel bad about themselves and significantly increase their risk of eating disorders.'

The publication of the College's new position paper on pro-ana websites coincides with the start of London Fashion Week (18-22 September 2009).

Professor Schmidt said: 'Pro-ana websites normalise illness. In much the same way, the catwalks of international fashion events such as London Fashion Week can act as a showcase for underweight women. We are very concerned that the lack of medical checks for models at London Fashion Week, coupled with working in an environment where being underweight is considered the norm, prevents models with eating disorders from gaining insight into their condition.'

Professor Schmidt also urged the fashion industry to take a lead in promoting a wider range of body images. Commenting on the 'All Walks Beyond the Catwalk' fashion showcase taking place at London's Somerset House tonight, Professor Schmidt said: 'It is vital that the fashion industry promotes more diverse body imagery, and we applaud the British Fashion Council for this ground-breaking event. We hope the event will start a dialogue and promote greater diversity within the fashion industry.'

The Eating Disorders Section also welcomes the Liberal Democrat's new Real Women policy, which makes six key recommendations relating to body image.

18 September 2009

⇨ The above information is reprinted with kind permission from the Royal College of Psychiatrists. Visit www.rcpsych.ac.uk for more information.

© Royal College of Psychiatrists

Pro-eating disorder websites

Information from SANE

SANE

A research paper, *Pro-Eating Disorder Websites: Users' Opinions*, written by SANE researchers was published in the *European Eating Disorders Review*.

The survey of 151 individuals, the first of its kind in the UK, aimed to discover who visits these sites and why, as well as examining the impact the sites have on those using them and whether they are perceived as helpful or damaging. Over a period of several months in 2005, 151 individuals took part in an online survey.

Key research findings

⇨ Almost 70 per cent of respondents were aged 22 or younger.

⇨ More than half of those surveyed visited pro-eating disorder websites at least once a day.

⇨ 24 per cent reported some kind of social difficulty.

⇨ 43 per cent said the sites were a source of emotional support.

'Concern'

With the growth of the Internet over the last decade this relatively new phenomenon has attracted much critical attention in the media. Concern has been expressed for the vulnerable people who may visit these websites in order to 'learn how to be anorexic' or to sustain disordered eating behaviour.

Most commonly these sites are hosted by people who themselves have an eating disorder. On the 'pro-ana' sites, for anorexia, or 'pro-mia', for bulimia, visitors can access 'Thinspirations' comprising anti-food or anti-fat slogans and photographs of thin celebrities and others in various types of emaciation. Alternatively, there are 'Tips or Tricks' on how to maintain disordered eating behaviour and keep them hidden from family and friends.

'Some visitors were as young as 13'

According to our study the visitors are mostly young and female. Some were as young as 13 and the majority were 22 or younger. Many visited the sites frequently, 41 per cent several times a day.

It has been suggested in the media that a distinguishing feature of the pro-eating disorder community is viewing anorexia or bulimia as a lifestyle rather than a disorder. When asked to reflect on this, 54 per cent of participants state unequivocally that an eating disorder was just that, a disorder. They described how their eating disorder affected how they experience the world, and themselves, and influencing their every perception, action and thought. This concept of lifestyle does not imply choice and is compatible with thinking of eating disorders as the damaging psychological disorder we know them to be.

'Many turn to the sites for friendship and support'

By its nature, an eating disorder can be very hard for others to understand and tends to put considerable distance between the sufferer and their family and friends. For nearly two-thirds of those surveyed, visiting the sites made them feel less lonely and isolated. This was most prevalent amongst the more frequent users who tended to make use of chat rooms and message boards. They reported improved self-esteem, feeling better about themselves and feeling less lonely. For many, the sites became a virtual community they could turn to for friendship and support.

'Harder to break away and seek recovery'

However, negative effects were also present and participants reported weighing, measuring, fasting and purging more often after visiting the sites. For some there was evidence the sites reinforced their identity as an anorexic or bulimic, making it harder for them to break away and seek recovery. 'There's a feeling one daren't recover, because then you'd

no longer belong', said one.

Just as disturbing was that passive browsers, those who visit the sites without utilising char rooms or contacting others, were more likely to view the sites as somewhere to go to become a 'better anorexic', and missed out on the beneficial social effects.

'Vulnerable people'

With 70 per cent of those who took part in the research reporting suicidal thoughts or feelings and 46 per cent also self-harming, visitors to these sites are clearly a very vulnerable group of people. Our concern is that the sites encourage visitors to hold on to their illness, supporting them in a pattern of damaging behaviour without encouraging them to seek treatment.

We have called for those publishing the sites to review their content and for ISPs to remove them, but in reality they are not simply going to go away. Indeed, removal of this form of social support, however loaded with dangers, could have unintended negative consequences.

At the heart of the pro-eating disorder community is the idea that an eating disorder can be of benefit to the person who has it. Constructive as it is, the current 'size zero' debate is in danger of reinforcing the belief that being thin is the only reason for clinging on to these illnesses. Other benefits, such as a feeling of safety or a sense of control are mentioned more frequently than any relating to appearance.

There can be no full understanding of the 'pro-ana' movement without further examination of this perception of benefit, a perception that from the 'normal' perspective seems irrational, but from that of an anorexic of bulimic can be fundamental.

The research paper *Pro-Eating Disorder Websites: Users' Opinions* by Emese Csipke and Outi Horne was published by the *European Eating Disorders Review* in spring 2007.
10 February 2009

⇨ The above information is reprinted with kind permission from SANE. Visit www.sane.org.uk for more.
© SANE

Too fat to be a princess?

Information from the British Psychological Society

Even before they start school, many young girls worry that they are fat. But a new study published in the *British Journal of Developmental Psychology* suggests the stereotypically thin and beautiful Disney princesses may not be a cause of children's anxieties.

During the study by Professor Stacey Tantleff-Dunn and doctoral student Sharon Hayes at the University of Central Florida, 121 girls aged three to six were asked how they felt about the way they look. Half of the girls then watched parts of animated children's movies that featured young, beautiful characters and appearance-focused comments, such as Gaston telling Belle in *Beauty and the Beast* that she is 'the most beautiful girl in town, and that makes her the best'. The second group watched parts of animated children's movies that did not contain any appearance-related messages, such as *Dora the Explorer*.

The children were then asked questions about what a real princess is, and their behaviour was monitored as they played in a room that featured fancy dress costumes, a mirror and other toys.

During the initial conversation, 31 per cent of the girls indicated they almost always worry about their appearance, while another 18 per cent said they sometimes worry about it. 30 per cent of the girls said they would change a physical attribute, such as their weight or hair colour.

However, exposure to the Disney films and appearance-focused comments within did not affect the girls' body dissatisfaction or engagement in appearance-related play behaviours. The majority of the girls, 99, still believed they could be a princess regardless of their weight, and their age.

The UCF study concluded that young girls did not appear to be influenced by repeated exposure to the beautiful, thin princesses in animated children's movies. 'While older girls and women tend to compare themselves to the models, younger children may be more likely to adopt the persona of the princesses while playing,' the UCF researchers said.

However, the high number of the girls worried about being fat at such a young age concerned the researchers.

'We do need to help our children challenge the images of beauty, particularly thinness, that they see and idolise and encourage them to question how much appearance should be part of their self-worth,' said Tantleff-Dunn. 'We should help them build a positive self-image with an appreciation for many different types of body attributes.'
27 November 2009

⇨ The above information is reprinted with kind permission from the British Psychological Society. Visit www.bps.org.uk for more information.

© British Psychological Society

Anorexia risk 'could be predicted'

Study suggests that subtle differences in brain development in womb can increase vulnerability

Thousands of girls are pre-disposed to develop anorexia because of the way their brains developed in the womb, says a major new study.

The report's authors say children could be screened at the age of eight to identify the signs that make them more vulnerable to risk factors such as the size zero fad and the cult of the super-thin celebrity. Eating disorder charities said the findings, which will be revealed at a conference at the Institute of Education in London this week, could revolutionise the treatment of anorexia.

Children could be screened at the age of eight to identify the signs that make them more vulnerable to risk factors

'Our research shows that certain kids' brains develop in such a way that makes them more vulnerable to the more commonly-known risk factors for eating disorders, such as the size-zero debate, media representations of very skinny women and bad parents,' said Ian Frampton, one of the authors, who is an honorary consultant in paediatric psychology at London's Great Ormond Street hospital.

Frampton and his colleagues conducted in-depth neuropsychological testing on more than 200 people in the UK, America and Norway who suffer from the condition. Almost all of those who took part in the study were girls and young women aged between 12 and 25 who were being treated for anorexia at private hospitals in Edinburgh and Maidenhead that are part of the Huntercombe medical group.

By Denis Campbell, health correspondent

They found that about 70% of the patients had suffered damage to their neurotransmitters (which help brain cells communicate with each other), had undergone subtle changes in the structure of their brains, or both.

One in every few hundred girls may be affected in this way, according to Frampton, who said the condition was random and not the result of poor maternal diet or environmental factors, such as widespread use of chemicals. Imperfect wiring in the brain's insular cortex that may lead to dyslexia, ADHD or depression in other children produces what he calls 'an underlying vulnerability' among some young people that makes them more likely to develop anorexia.

Previously, scientists believed that being chronically underweight caused changes in a person's brain. This new research is significant because it suggests that the opposite process explains the origins of anorexia. 'These findings could help us to understand this beguiling disease that we don't know how to treat,' added Frampton.

'Arguments that social factors such as girls feeling under pressure to lose weight in order to look like high-profile women in the media contain logical flaws because almost everyone is exposed to them, yet only a small percentage of young people get anorexia.

'Those things are important but there must be other factors, involving genetics and science, that make some young people much more vulnerable than others.'

Between 2% and 3% of children and young adults develop an eating disorder. Anorexia is the rarest of them. About four women in every thousand develop it. Cases among men are rare but not unknown. It can lead to serious health problems and prove fatal. Karen Carpenter, the 1970s pop star, died in 1983 at the age of 32 from a heart attack brought on by the condition.

In recent years, the fashion industry has come under pressure to protect the health of its models following widespread anger about the size-zero trend and the deaths of two models. On the eve of a photographic shoot in November 2006, Brazilian model Ana Carolina Reston died from complications arising from anorexia. It was reported that she had been living on a diet of apples and tomatoes. It followed the death that summer of Uruguayan model, Luisel Ramos, who died of heart failure at the age of 22 after not eating for several days in an attempt to stay thin.

Susan Ringwood, chief executive of the leading eating disorders charity, beat, welcomed the latest research.

'It could pave the way for the first drugs to be developed to treat eating disorders, similar to the way that anti-depressants help rebalance the brain of people with depression,' she said.

'And it will help parents understand that they aren't to blame. Parents always blame themselves when their child develops an eating disorder. But what we are learning more and more from research in this area is that some people are very vulnerable to anorexia and that is down to genetic factors and brain chemistry, and not them trying to look like celebrity models or suffering a major traumatic event early in their lives.

'This research is a key missing part of the jigsaw of our understanding of anorexia.'

29 March 2009

What are the treatments for eating disorders?

Information from Rethink

Many people with an eating disorder will deny that anything is wrong if some one tries to confront the issue. If they are determined not to talk about it, you could suggest that they at least read a little about eating disorders to help them recognise their own situation. They may even be relieved that it is a recognised condition for which there is support and treatment.

Teaching individuals new coping strategies is often part of therapy plans

When someone with an eating disorder gets to a level of acceptance of their situation where they want to change, treatment will aim to restore regular and healthy eating patterns, and deal with psychological and emotional issues. Teaching individuals new coping strategies is often part of therapy plans. Your first step is usually through your GP, who can begin the referral process onto specialists and treatments as needed.

There are a number of different types of treatments for eating disorders, and people may be offered a combination of these.

⇨ For those at a very low weight, the first stage will focus on getting weight put on, before therapy begins. This may be done as an in-patient at a hospital or specialist facility.

⇨ Talking therapies are often an important part of eating disorder treatments and may include: counselling, cognitive behaviour therapy (CBT), interpersonal therapy (IPT), group therapy, and family therapy.

⇨ Family support to address as a family any issues which may have led to the eating disorder and to support the family as a whole.

⇨ In some cases medication may be prescribed, such as antidepressants, but medication should not be the only treatment for eating disorders.

For some people who are at a severely low body weight and in a dangerous physical condition, compulsory admission may be used through sectioning under the Mental Health Act. This can be very distressing for people with anorexia, as feeling in control is such an important need for them. Hospitalisation should only ever be part of a wider approach which addresses reasons for the disorder developing in the first place. The most suitable treatment for an individual depends on their age, weight and situation.

According to the Royal College of Psychiatrists, more than half of people with anorexia recover after being ill for an average period of five to six years. Studies suggest that one in five of the most severe cases of anorexia may be fatal, though this rate is much lower if a person stays in touch with medical care. As long as the heart and other organs are not damaged, the other complications caused by starvation will improve slowly when the person is eating again. Total recovery from bulimia is more difficult to achieve, although therapy can help a person gain more control over the disorder and their life. Cognitive behaviour therapy seems to work more quickly than other types of therapy for bulimia. *Updated June 2009*

⇨ The above information is reprinted with kind permission from Rethink. Visit www.rethink.org for more information.

© *Rethink*

SELF-LOATHING

DOUBT

LACK OF TRUST

NEVER THIN ENOUGH

You've taken the most important step in recovery.

Eating disorders in teenagers

Information from Anorexia and Bulimia Care

Dieting

Dieting is very common amongst teenagers (especially girls) and some may even do things like skipping meals, making themselves sick, or even taking diet pills in an attempt to control their weight. However, those who are developing real problems tend to be much more strict about their diets, for example only eating a very narrow or 'safe' set of foods, and showing very little flexibility in their diet. They may also show signs of distress or panic if they ever do break the diet or are in a situation where they might have to eat food that is not on their 'safe' list.

Weight loss should always be taken seriously, so if you are concerned, do seek advice

Weight loss

Weight loss is unfortunately also quite common as so many teenagers do diet. However, in general, teenagers under 16 years and of course younger children should not be losing weight unless they really need to do so – and in this case a GP or dietitian should supervise it. Weight loss should always be taken seriously, so if you are concerned, do seek advice.

Changes in mood

Changes in mood are also a common sign of eating disorders. Often children who develop problems have previously been very helpful, kind and polite. The development of an eating disorder can transform them into quiet, withdrawn and depressed children, who may react in defensive, angry or even violent ways to your enquiries about their eating. They may also become very secretive, or lie to you about what they have and have not eaten.

It is important to remember that these changes are caused by the eating disorder, they are not part of your child's character, and are a sign of the distress that s/he is feeling. Other signs may be evident as well that all is not well. Many children exercise excessively, and this may well be done in secret, perhaps before you get up in the morning, or after you go to bed at night.

You might find your child making excuses for not eating or trying to avoid meals or you might realise that they always go to the bathroom directly after eating. Your child may show other physical signs, such as being constantly cold, or having difficulty sleeping. In girls, periods may stop, or not start. Overall, the rule is that if you are concerned, do seek further advice.

How to approach?

One of the most common questions we receive at ACHE is from a parent/family member who is concerned about a child/teenager and is seeking advice about how to approach them about what is going on. It can be very tricky, and a lot of teenagers in particular react very defensively to any kind of questioning about their health, weight or eating.

We would offer two main pieces of advice for the moment – but if you are in this situation then do get in touch and we can offer you more specific guidance. We also have some very useful guide booklets to help you. Please see the Anorexia Bulimia Care publications page at www.anorexiabulimiacare.co.uk/publications

Avoid challenging them about their eating/weight

The aggressive, defensive responses which you are trying to avoid stem mostly from the fear of losing control over eating, or of being made to change eating habits and gain weight. A lot of sufferers feel that all the people around them want them to do is just get fatter and stop causing trouble.

It is really important that you show that you are concerned about much more than this – about how they are feeling in general. For this reason, if you can, it is better to start off by talking to them about some of the other changes you have noticed, and how they are feeling in themselves. So if you have noticed a change to their mood, or emotions, or to things that they used to enjoy doing, this is a much better thing to start to talk about. Be empathetic and sympathetic, and view this first chat as a chance to start communicating. You may not even get to mention the weight/eating issue in this first chat and that is fine. You need to get their confidence, and make it clear that you are on their side.

Do not confront

When talking to someone who is struggling with an eating disorder you have to remember that for them life has become lived on a knife-edge of anxiety. If therefore they feel that in any way you are pushing them, or trying to take control from them, they are likely to react by digging their heels in and refusing to cooperate. They will also be likely to feel that you, like everyone else, are against them. For this reason, avoid being confrontational when you chat to them. Instead adopt as relaxed a style as you can, and try to gain as much understanding as possible about how they are feeling. So avoid statements like 'Well you just need to eat a bit better, don't you!' and try to use things like 'So you want to eat a bit better but feel really scared about losing control, is that right?'.

Remember that your first aim is to get communication open, and to give them some support because they are probably feeling dreadful

---

You may still find that they become emotional and tense – and if this happens you might want to withdraw and maybe start up the conversation at another time. Most of all, avoid the temptation to give in to your own fears and try to take control. This is a very understandable response, particularly if the child is younger – but often is counterproductive and just makes things worse. Remember that your first aim is to get communication open, and to give them some support because they are probably feeling dreadful.

If all else fails ...

It may be that you have already tried to approach your child and it has failed, or that you feel you do not have the right kind of relationship with them to be able to approach them. If this is the case then do consider whether there is someone else who might be better placed to talk to them – perhaps a trusted teacher, friend or aunt. Be very careful, however, about who you decide to tell, as it is vital that your child does not feel that they are being talked about. It is much better if the person who does speak to them has already noticed what is going on themselves.

If your child is very defensive and you find you are unable to say anything to them at all without being shouted at, one thing that sometimes works is to use short notes or cards. You can leave a note/card somewhere where they will find it, even at a time when they will be unable to immediately come and shout at you. This means you can be totally non-confrontational, and that if your child finds it impossible to talk to you face to face, s/he does have another way of communicating. You can suggest in the note that they reply by another note, and where they could leave it for you. Some parents have even agreed in the note that they will never mention these issues face to face unless the child brings it up first. All of this helps them to feel really secure and in control – but does ensure that some form of communication begins.

⇨ The above information is reprinted with kind permission from Anorexia and Bulimia Care (ABC). Visit www. anorexiabulimiacare.co.uk for more information.

© Anorexia and Bulimia Care (ABC)

Helpful dos and don'ts

We have much advice and many suggestions we can discuss with you personally to suit your particular situation and we have many good publications that enable us to help you further.

Here are some main points to consider:

DO
- ⇨ Empathise with them – be clear that you understand how they feel.
- ⇨ Let them correct you if they feel you have not quite under-stood.
- ⇨ Let them talk.
- ⇨ Try to focus on how they are feeling, NOT on what they are or are not eating.
- ⇨ Help find a way that they can see their GP. Perhaps it would help if you made the appointment, went along first alone and then went with them – or even if you spoke for them.
- ⇨ Emphasise that you are in this with them and that you will work with them to help them to feel better and happier.

DON'T
- ⇨ Issue ultimatums (e.g. 'if you don't go to the doctor I will tell your teachers/friend/husband/wife what is going on').
- ⇨ Tell lots of people unnecessarily.
- ⇨ Use emotional blackmail (e.g. 'Do you know what this is doing to me?').
- ⇨ Get caught up in endless arguments about issues sur-rounding food and weight – for example, whether they are or are not fat, whether eating certain foods would or would not make them fat. It is pointless and will probably just end up with both of you frustrated, upset and fed up!
- ⇨ Focus on food and weight too much. For example, make sure you talk about recovery in terms of how they are feeling, and how they are coping with their life rather than in terms of normalising eating, stabilising weight or putting weight on.

Self-help tips

Information from Disordered Eating

If you or someone you know is living with an eating disorder, there is no substitute for professional help. Eating disorders that go on for many months should be investigated by a qualified health professional. However, there are things people who suffer from eating disorders can do to help themselves.

Developing healthy relationships with food, exercise and your own body is an essential part of the recovery/prevention process of any pattern of disordered eating, so here are some basic self-help tips.

Eat regular meals

Eating three meals a day including breakfast, lunch and dinner is a good place to start. Some people prefer to eat five or six smaller meals each day; this is fine, but remember it is your overall calorie intake each day that is important (2,500 kcal for men and 2,000 kcal for women). Try to avoid skipping meals and do not wait until you are starving, as you are more likely to overeat at your next meal. Choose healthy snacks such as fruit, nuts and yoghurt in between meals if you are hungry.

Eat meals with family or friends

A person who is anxious about eating will feel more comfortable doing so among other people they trust, such as family or friends. This may mean planning ahead to ensure meals are served at times when everyone can be present. Try to keep the topic of conversation positive throughout each meal, and avoid talking about food, particularly calories and fat content. Meal times are a good opportunity for a person with an eating disorder to learn to associate eating with a pleasant environment.

Eat healthy foods

The types of foods we eat are important. We all like to indulge in our favourite foods every once in a while, but we should also eat as wide a variety of healthy, nutritious foods as possible. General nutrition guidelines include:

⇨ Eating plenty of fruits and vegetables.

⇨ Choosing complex carbohydrates such as bread, rice and pasta (whole grain if possible) rather than processed sugars.

⇨ Eating protein in the form of lean meats, fish, poultry, legumes and nuts.

⇨ Drinking water regularly.

Avoid weighing yourself and looking in the mirror

If you can bring yourself to, throw the scales away, or weigh yourself no more than once a week. What the scales say is not an indication of how good a person you are, and you do not need their approval. Continual weighing and scrutinising yourself in the mirror is not going to help you free yourself from your insecurities about your weight and body image. There are matters more worthy of your attention, such as family, friends and other things you have going on in your life.

Keep a food diary

Keep a food diary of what you eat and when you eat it to help you focus on eating regularly. Also record any episodes of going without food for long periods of time, bingeing or purging and the thoughts and emotions you have about them. If you can learn to recognise the situations and feelings that lead you to engage in unhealthy eating behaviours it will help you to figure out ways of dealing with them. The things you find out about yourself may surprise you.

Take regular exercise

Studies have shown exercise to have a positive effect on low self-esteem and poor body image, which are widely cited as being contributory factors in the onset of eating disorders. Remember exercise is good for us, but too much can have a detrimental effect and place unnecessary stress on our bodies. People with anorexia often have a compulsion to exercise excessively and this needs to be addressed. A healthy amount is 30 minutes of physical activity on five days of the week.

Be patient

Unhealthy relationships with food do not develop overnight, and it can take many months and even years to regain full control over your eating habits. The road to recovery is a long one along which you must be prepared to take small steps, but you have every chance of making it. Remember, if you have acknowledged you have a problem and have resolved yourself to doing something about it, you are already halfway there.

⇨ The above information is reprinted with kind permission from Disordered Eating. Visit www.disordered-eating. co.uk for more information.

© Disordered Eating

Bye, bye scales!

Obesity leaves eating disorders in the shade

While national guidelines have stimulated change in crisis areas of mental health, eating disorders are only just beginning to receive the attention and specialist services sufferers need

By Alison Moore

Obesity is never out of the headlines at the moment; what was once a personal matter is now seen as public health enemy number one.

But does the current obsession with fat mean the NHS is ignoring the needs of those with other eating disorders – such as anorexia – and could the portrayal of the UK as a nation of fatties even be adding to the problems?

Some doctors are nervous about the increasing concentration on obesity, feeling that vulnerable young people could misinterpret some of the messages.

The weighing of children when they first join school and again in the last year of primary school is now being strengthened with parents sent letters warning if their children are overweight.

But Robin Arnold of the British Medical Association's psychiatrists committee warned of some of the consequences when this was first mooted two years ago, telling one newspaper: 'It may well be justified in public health terms but one wonders what it will do to rates of eating disorders in the future.'

beat – the eating disorders association – is also aware that obesity messages could have unfortunate consequences and has been working with the Government on tempering some of the messages in publicity material. Its annual report warns: 'Children who are bullied about their weight and shape are particularly vulnerable.'

'The campaign against obesity is a double-edged sword,' says John Morgan, secretary of the Royal College of Psychiatry eating disorders section, who has been working in schools on body image issues. 'It could even do harm.'

'Some of the messages will be detrimental to people with eating disorders,' says beat spokeswoman Mary George. 'All the attention paid to calorific values and what we put in our body... it's exactly the message we don't want.'

And John Evans, a professor of sociology at Loughborough University, has carried out research on the impact of anti-obesity campaigns on adolescents; this showed that it could inadvertently lead to more concern about their weight and potentially propel them towards a damaging relationship with food.

Unintended consequences

The Department of Health (DH) says its obesity strategy focuses on promoting healthy weight, achieved through positive attitudes towards a balanced diet and regular physical activity.

'We are working with experts to help ensure that there are no unintended consequences of our communications,' a spokeswoman says. She adds the DH is funding research on anorexia through the National Institute for Health Research.

But one thing is clear: while obesity may be a long-term risk to health, eating disorders – principally anorexia – are an immediate threat. Anorexia has the highest death rate of any psychological disorder, with 10–20 per cent of untreated anorexics dying from it. Yet it can sometimes be difficult for people to get help, even when they are willing to acknowledge the condition.

This was cruelly brought home by the inquest earlier this month into the death of teenager Charlotte Robinson, whose body mass index was only 11 when she died from pneumonia.

Reluctant to have in-patient treatment, she was eventually admitted to a private clinic used by the NHS, but her condition deteriorated and she later died in an acute hospital.

The coroner who delivered a narrative verdict on her death earlier this month said there had been 'inappropriate delays' which reduced the likelihood of recovery. Both Norfolk primary care trust and the mental health trust concerned have said they take the findings very seriously and, although some changes have already been made, they will look at what else needs to be done.

But are there wider problems with eating disorder services? Dr Morgan says provision is patchy and inadequate, and some areas pay only lip service to National Institute for Health and Clinical Excellence (NICE) guidelines.

Political issue

It is hard to get figures for the number of people with eating disorders. Some put it as high as 1.1 million. Former deputy prime minister John Prescott, who recently admitted he had suffered from bulimia, had asked for statistics to be gathered on prevalence but this request was turned down by the Department of Health.

London and the South are generally better served for specialist services than elsewhere but this may hide local differences.

A review of services under way in the East of England has found substantial differences in in-patient admission rates, for example, although this is linked to what level of community provision is provided.

beat says there is little consistency. 'We are seeing more units open but not enough,' says Ms George. 'We are lobbying the Government and the DH that eating disorders should be higher on the mental health agenda.'

It is not easy, either, to be certain that services follow NICE guidelines, issued in 2004. NICE itself does not monitor implementation and there is no time limit or obligation to adopt them.

Dr Morgan fears mental health services are increasingly concentrating on patients perceived as a risk to others rather than themselves alone. 'There's a tendency to be dismissive about eating disorders,' he says. 'But it has a higher death rate than schizophrenia. Psychiatry is at risk of becoming an agent of social control.'

Local practice

The first port of call for any sufferer – or sometimes their family and friends – is likely to be a GP.

In some cases GPs will deal with the problem themselves or monitor the patient for some weeks. They may refer patients to a community mental health team, where there will be varying levels of knowledge about eating disorders. Severe cases will need specialist input and possibly inpatient admission.

But Dr Morgan says: 'It can take people a long time to access specialist treatment and a lot of lobbying and campaigning on their behalf. I have known cases where families have gone to their local MPs to get specialist treatment.'

Norfolk PCT, which is awaiting the outcome of a review of eating disorders commissioning by NHS East of England, is now likely to commission pathways that lead to quicker specialist input.

This could reduce the need for inpatient beds: there is evidence that patients seen in a specialist service are far less likely to end up being admitted to hospital. Patients with anorexia have a median length of stay of 36 days, so services that reduce the chances of that happening could save money.

Mark Weston, assistant director of commissioning at Norfolk PCT, also expects that any changes could uncover unmet need. He would like to see increased prevention and promotion, which could create opportunities for early intervention, when outcomes are far better.

But in many places specialist services are still being developed.

The DH spokeswoman says responsibility for provision of treatment rests with PCTs but acknowledges that specialised tertiary services are available from 'relatively few providers'.

Kathy Chapman, locality manager with Norfolk and Waveney Mental Health foundation trust, says areas have responded to national guidance on mental health by setting up crisis intervention and other teams, but are only now focusing on more specialist services, including eating disorders.

'There has been massive transformation in mental health but eating disorders has not been the top of the list,' says Ms Chapman, and many trusts are at the stage of adding more highly specialist services. 'What is starting to happen now is that we are identifying a range of specialist functions which community mental health teams need to develop.'

In the longer term, the trust wants to develop a specialist eating disorders service with a consultant, psychologist and psychotherapists; this could also provide support for GPs and community mental health teams working with less severe cases.

Added angst

Across the East of England, spending on eating disorders has been increasing at 30 per cent, says Jess Lievesley of the strategic health authority's public health team. The current review, prompted by access and waiting time promises in the region's response to the next stage review – is likely to lead to more consistent community services and potentially less use of in-patient beds.

In many areas, patients may have to travel more than 50 miles to access specialist services, many of which are provided by the private sector: three years ago 33 per cent of the then 29 SHAs had no specialist treatment services and only 14 per cent of patients were treated close to home. The situation may have improved since then, but provision is still patchy, says beat. Very few units will carry out nasogastric feeding – so patients are either transferred to the acute sector or face even longer journeys.

'Young and fragile people are having to travel some distance to access treatment, which just adds to the angst they are experiencing and is a hell of a strain on the family,' says Ms George. beat's research suggests 79 per cent of families feel they suffer lasting damage from eating disorders

and only 12 per cent feel they get all the support they need. The need for support and information for families was stressed in the NICE guidelines yet 82 per cent of interviewed families were not offered any literature by GPs.

Day care is proving successful, even in severe cases, says Dr Morgan, but it is difficult to provide outside big centres of population. Hub-and-spoke approaches where specialists work closely with community teams can help: for example, a community psychiatric nurse could be trained to deliver cognitive behavioural therapy to patients with mild bulimia.

The point of release from hospital is also a concern: if services are not well developed, then clinicians may be reluctant to discharge a patient, adding to long lengths of stay. Better services in the community and a planned care pathway for discharged patients could address this.

Dr Morgan suggests that commissioning could incentivise sustainable recovery.

Many anorexia sufferers are teenagers, and may fall between services for children and for adults. Research by beat three years ago suggested only 17 per cent of young people were treated in an appropriate setting, although this may have improved since then.

There can also be problems if they need to transfer from child and adolescent services into adult services: in some cases, there have been age gaps between the two (one finishing at 16 and the other starting at 18) and also a difference in the philosophy and approach to care.

Adult tertiary-level eating disorders will come under the new specialised commissioning groups in each SHA area from April, recognising these are low-volume but high-cost services which need to look beyond PCT boundaries.

20 November 2008

⇨ The above information is reprinted with kind permission from the *Health Service Journal*. Visit the HSJ website at www.hsj.co.uk for more information on this and other related topics.

© *Health Service Journal*

'While I was eating I would go into a trance'

Sophie Todd, 25, from Surrey used to eat anything she could lay her hands on. Now she has a much healthier relationship with food. She describes how she overcame a binge-eating disorder

'I was very young, about 11, when I felt that the relationship I had with food was not the same as my friends', and I thought it strange that I was so much larger than a lot of children my age.

'I put on more weight and was obsessed with food. I was always eating. I had a very low self-esteem and no self-confidence, both of which made life very difficult. As a result, I started to eat more as that was my comfort and escape.

'I would eat large quantities of anything I could in short periods of time. While I was eating I would go into a trance and didn't realise the quantities I was consuming. I had no control and couldn't stop.

'Despite desperately wanting help, I didn't have anyone I could turn to. Friends tried to approach me about it, but I would say I had a slow metabolism and my family ate large amounts. I also used to say the stress of growing up made me feel hungry all the time.

'My family were not very supportive. I think it was because a lot of them are big. People at school used to laugh at me and make fun of my size. They called me names and said I was lazy and greedy.

'I had a lot of family and emotional issues and eating was my way of controlling feelings around them. Eventually, I decided to do something about my problem and spent five weeks at Life Works' residential facility in Surrey, which changed my life in so many ways.

'We had three meals a day and were not allowed seconds, which helped me to realise what a normal quantity of food is. We did art therapy and a lot of group work learning about nutrition.

'I learned to deal with my feelings (identifying and expressing them healthily), which I had not done for as long as I could remember. At last, I had found a safe and loving environment where it was OK to talk about my past or where I could think about my past and why I used food in the way I did. I learned so much about how to cope with my relationship with food.

'I was up and down through my stay, but that was all part of the journey. It was a grieving process; losing a best friend but at the same time being free of your worst enemy. I felt raw emotionally and tired and drained but, in time, those feelings turned to positive thoughts full of hope for the future.

'I'm constantly aware of my feelings now and careful not to fall into old traps. Although I occasionally still feel emotionally immature and fragile, I generally feel more able to enjoy and make the most of life and the opportunities it offers at me.'

23 January 2009

⇨ The above information is reprinted with kind permission from NHS Choices. Visit www.nhs.uk for more information on this and other related issues.

© *NHS Choices*

Choice or chance?

Ending the information lottery

The NHS Constitution promises a health service based on choice, information and respect – and beat welcomes this commitment. However, for people affected by eating disorders, their experience of the health service too often falls far short of this. beat surveyed 1,500 people affected by an eating disorder about their experiences of visiting their GP. The vast majority encountered uninformed GPs and a widespread lack of understanding. Rather than 'choice', their recovery was entirely down to chance – with the odds stacked against them.

Chance: the 'information lottery'

59% of people visit their GP about their eating disorder worries. beat always encourages people to speak to their GP about their eating disorder. Speaking out ends the silence and secrecy on which eating disorders thrive. It is a courageous step – and a great first move towards recovery.

'My GP referred me straight away to the nearest mental health unit. The help I got was immeasurable. Not once did I feel a burden or that I wasn't worth bothering about. I'm lucky to live near one of the best GPs.'

But people need to have confidence and trust that their GP is informed about eating disorders and knows how to help them. beat knows that an understanding and supportive GP can be a gateway to effective treatment – and a signpost to recovery. Yet according to our survey only 15% of people felt their GP understood eating disorders and knew how to help.

'I felt as if my weight had to drop before the GP would take my worries seriously.'

Far too many people encounter a GP who is not up to date about eating disorders. We have heard from people whose GPs did not take eating disorders seriously, treating it as a phase or a diet gone wrong. GPs should be putting an end to these dangerous myths – not propagating them.

'When I first went to see my GP they didn't listen at all. They just told me it was a phase I was going through.'

The majority of people told us their GP was unable to help them: GPs didn't know about available treatment or how they could access it. People affected by eating disorders need support, provided without delay. If GPs aren't informed about available treatment then their patients' recovery can be endangered – with fatal consequences.

'I left the doctors feeling disheartened, patronised and as if I was making a big fuss about nothing.'

beat is committed to bring about change, and improving the choices that everyone has about their health. The NHS has promised a service based on choice, not on chance. Our major campaigning issue for 2009 is to hold the NHS to their promise.

'People with eating disorders should be assessed and receive treatment at the earliest opportunity.'
The NICE guidelines on eating disorders

Ending the lottery: a campaign for choice

The NICE guidelines on eating disorders provide evidence-based recommendations of effective treatment. They state that recovery is possible, provided that GPs listen to their patients, act quickly and, in the case of young people, involve their families as much as possible.

'You have the right to choice about your NHS care and to information to support these choices.'
The NHS Constitution

The NHS Constitution grants patients a legal right to the treatment NICE recommends. GPs are crucial to this right becoming a reality. Our campaign will hold the health service to account. We will champion best practice and highlight where changes are needed. We call on the NHS to do away with the unacceptable variety in standards of primary care.

That only 15% of our survey felt their GPs to be informed and understanding is a shocking indictment of just how much needs to be done.

Choosing recovery

'My GP phoned me the next morning and told me he'd referred me to a specialist eating disorder service.'

beat wants to see the NHS deliver their promise. We want anyone affected by an eating disorder to feel able to speak to their GP, confident they will reach someone who understands their condition and is willing to listen.

'I was happy to open up to my GP. She made it feel as if I could – because she was there to help me.'

Right now, too few people receive the quality of service that should be theirs by right – rather than by luck or chance. It is only by ending this information lottery that everyone will have the best chance of beating their eating disorder.

'My GP discussed the different options for treatment – she told me about counselling and other services I could be referred to. She explained how long the referral would take. I left feeling relieved and comfortable – and optimistic about recovery.'

23 February 2009

⇨ The above information is reprinted with kind permission from beat. Visit www.b-eat.co.uk for more.

© beat

Psychotherapy for eating disorders

New psychotherapy has potential to treat majority of cases of eating disorders

Wellcome Trust researchers have developed a new form of psychotherapy that has been shown to have the potential to treat more than eight out of ten cases of eating disorders in adults, a study out today reports.

This new 'enhanced' form of cognitive behavioural therapy (CBT-E) builds on and improves the current leading treatment for bulimia nervosa as recommended by the National Institute of Health and Clinical Excellence (NICE). CBT-E is the first treatment to be shown to be suitable for the majority of cases of eating disorders.

According to NICE, eating disorders are a major cause of physical and psychosocial impairment in young women, affecting at least one in 20 women between the ages of 18 and 30. They also occur in young men but are less common. Three eating disorders are recognised: anorexia nervosa, which accounts for around one in ten cases in adults; bulimia nervosa, which accounts for a third of all cases; and the remainder are classed as atypical eating disorders, which account for over half of all cases. In these atypical cases the features of anorexia nervosa and bulimia nervosa are combined in a different way.

The three eating disorders vary in their severity, but typically involve extreme and relentless dieting, self-induced vomiting or laxative misuse, binge eating, driven exercising and in some cases marked weight loss. Common associated features are depression, social withdrawal, perfectionism and low self-esteem. The disorders tend to run a chronic course and are notoriously difficult to treat. Relapse is common.

This new treatment derives from an earlier form of CBT that was designed exclusively for patients with bulimia nervosa. Both were

wellcometrust

developed by Professor Christopher Fairburn, a Wellcome Trust Principal Research Fellow at the University of Oxford. In 2004, the earlier treatment became the first psychotherapy to be recognised by NICE as the leading treatment for a clinical condition and its use was recommended across the NHS.

___

Approximately two-thirds of those who completed treatment made a complete and lasting response

___

Now, in a study published today in the *American Journal of Psychiatry*, Professor Fairburn and colleagues have shown that the enhanced version of the treatment is not only more potent than the earlier NICE-recommended treatment, but it can also be used to treat both bulimia nervosa and the atypical eating disorders, making it suitable for over 80 per cent of cases of eating disorders.

'Eating disorders are serious mental health problems and can be very distressing for both patients and their families,' says Professor Fairburn. 'Now for the first time, we have a single treatment that can be effective at treating the majority of cases without the need for patients to be admitted into hospital.'

154 people were recruited for the study, which was based in Oxfordshire and Leicestershire. Two versions of CBT-E were compared: a simple version that focused solely on the eating disorder and a second, more complex version that simultaneously addressed commonly associated problems such as low self-esteem and extreme perfectionism. Both treatments comprised 20 50-minute outpatient appointments over 20 weeks.

The researchers found that the majority of patients responded well and rapidly to the two forms of CBT-E and that the changes were sustained over the following year, the time at which relapse is most likely to occur. Approximately two-thirds of those who completed treatment made a complete and lasting response with many of the remainder showing substantial improvement. Patients with bulimia nervosa or an atypical eating disorder responded equally well, though a planned sub-analysis showed that patients with particularly complex clinical features responded better to the more complex treatment and vice versa.

'This new psychotherapy is an effective and relatively straightforward intervention for treating most clinical disorders seen in adults,' says Professor Fairburn. 'It is increasingly being used across the NHS and has the potential to improve the lives of the hundreds of thousands of people living with eating disorders.'

Professor Fairburn and colleagues are also nearing the completion of a large-scale trial investigating the effectiveness of CBT-E as a treatment for anorexia nervosa, the interim results of which look very promising.

The findings have been welcomed by Susan Ringwood, Chief Executive Officer of beat, the UK's eating disorders campaign group: 'This research shows that people can benefit from psychological therapy even at a very low weight. There has been so little research into eating disorders and anorexia in particular, and Professor Fairburn's work has really added to our knowledge in this challenging field.'

The research is the culmination of a seven-year study funded by the Wellcome Trust, the UK's largest medical research charity.
15 December 2008

⇨ The above information is reprinted with kind permission from the Wellcome Trust. Visit the Wellcome Trust website at www.wellcome.ac.uk for more information on this and other related topics.

© *Wellcome Trust*

An aching hunger

Hospital admissions for teenagers with anorexia have risen 80% over the last decade. Laurie Penny, who had the condition for years, explains why more help is needed for this most deadly of mental illnesses

In 2003, I was intent on avoiding mirrors. They were the enemy. They reflected back wasted limbs, yellow skin, teeth like tombstones in a scared, skull-like face. I was in the process of starving myself to death, and whatever had made me do it, as I skulked past the looking glass I knew it wasn't a yearning to be attractive.

I'm not the only woman who has tried to make herself disappear. Anorexia nervosa, the disorder of pathological self-starvation, is on the rise, with an 80% increase in hospital admissions among teenage girls over the last decade. Pressure groups and parents complain that there is still a chronic shortage of specialist care, with many GPs apparently reluctant to refer patients for treatment in the early stages of the disease. And this approach leaves children and their families to struggle on alone – usually until it is too late for simple intervention.

I was hospitalised with severe anorexia five years ago, when I was 17, and only now can I truly begin to understand the cruelties of my condition. Anorexia has the highest mortality rate of any mental illness, but it remains one of the least understood. It is estimated that between 8% and 20% of sufferers will die as a result of the condition – half

By Laurie Penny

of them by suicide – and that a further 30% will remain ill for life, with complications including osteoporosis, digestive diseases, chronic anxiety, psychosis and heart failure. One or two in every 100 young women and one in every 1,000 young men has the disease, although anorexia has been recorded in every age group.

> **One or two in every 100 young women and one in every 1,000 young men has the disease, although anorexia has been recorded in every age group**

Anorexia has long been trivialised as a by-product of celebrity and fashion culture, and this media focus has sharpened since the death of two models in 2006. But the condition is actually far more than that: anorexia has been recorded since the 12th

century as a psychotic strategy of self-control, which suggests that we have to look far beyond the pages of today's women's magazines for answers.

What anorexia often appears to offer is salvation from desire. My generation has grown up schooled like no other in the fine art of dissatisfaction – with our lives, our possessions and our bodies. For modern teenage girls the encouragement to do better, look better and have more can become almost unbearable. I have a visceral memory of lying on my bedroom floor after a particularly punishing exercise session, pounding the wall and sobbing 'I don't need anything! I don't want anything! I mustn't want anything!' I was desperate to destroy the aching need I felt, not just for an extra biscuit or square of chocolate, but for life and all of its adventure. This had nothing to do with wanting to look prettier, and everything to do with a process of shutting the doors on life one by one.

Like 30% of sufferers, Hannah, now 23, developed anorexia after experiencing sexual abuse as a child. 'I wanted to look disgusting and ugly,' she says. 'I wanted my heart to sputter and stop and my bones to thin, my organs to give up on me. Beyond everything, I think I just wanted the physical symptoms to kill me, so that

I wouldn't have to make the final decision. If I had a heart attack caused by starvation, maybe that wouldn't really count as suicide.'

Anorexia is a fight between brain and body, between what a teenager envisages as the rational, perfectible mind and a body that just won't do what it's told. We live in a world where young women are commanded to always look available, but never actually be so. If women's bodies are there to be consumed, our most drastic retaliation is to consume ourselves.

The action group beat believes that too few GPs take anorexia seriously, particularly in its early stages. Sam, now in her 20s, tried to seek help when she felt her disease spiralling out of control. 'I went to my GP quite early on and told her that I couldn't eat because I was scared of gaining weight, but she just told me to eat more nuts and gave me some vegetarian recipes. My overriding memory of that time was of being trapped in an endless black nightmare, with no visible way out.'

Anorexia nervosa is the most lethal of all mental illnesses precisely because its physical and psychological effects are so profoundly entangled. It has been conclusively proved that prolonged starvation can actually provoke many of the symptoms of anorexia nervosa, causing sufferers to obsess over food and become depressed, self-destructive and suicidal. In 1944, for instance, researchers at the University of Minnesota enlisted and systematically starved 36 conscientious objectors – all healthy adult men with no psychiatric problems. Over the course of a year, the men lost 25% of their body weight, and were then fed normally again – with staggering results. All of the participants quickly began to display unusual psychological symptoms. They became highly distressed, agitated and bewildered, and developed bizarre rituals around eating, collecting recipes and hoarding food obsessively – not just during the experiment but, in some cases, for the rest of their lives.

One of the participants, Harold, told researchers in 2006 that the experiment was highly distressing 'not only because of the physical discomfort, but because...food became

the one central and only thing really in one's life. I mean, if you went to a movie, you weren't particularly interested in the love scenes, but you noticed every time they ate and what they ate.' The men became extremely disturbed by the idea of weight gain, and their reactions included pathological self-harm. One participant amputated three of his own fingers with an axe.

In recent years, the Minnesota study has been invaluable to psychiatrists wishing to understand the psychology and physiology of anorexia nervosa. But despite a growing recognition that successful treatment must involve provision for both the disordered emotions and the damaged physiology of the anorexic teenager, the availability of such care is extremely limited. There are currently more than 100 potential patients for every place in the UK's specialist treatment centres, most of which are in private hospitals. This lack of effective provision is another reason why GPs are reluctant to make referrals, often delaying until the anorexic displays potentially fatal weight loss.

It took me nine months of inpatient treatment to piece together the fragments of my body and sanity, and a further three years to make a full recovery. I am very lucky to have received such excellent care. Nearly half of the UK's specialist care teams for anorexia are in the south of England, with none at all

in Wales and Northern Ireland. As such, patients are at the mercy of their postcode, and hospital admission on overstretched general wards is too often a matter of force-feeding followed by rapid discharge. While this physical rehabilitation may put the patient temporarily out of danger, it is useless without addressing her mental distress – and so hospital admission becomes a revolving door, with patients quickly starving themselves again on release. This pushes up the hospitalisation figures even further. Of the nine teenagers on my ward in 2004, only myself and a skeletal boy of 13 were on our first admission.

The high relapse rate points to a tragic waste of medical resources. If proper care were provided for more of Britain's anorexic teenagers, the disease could be treated effectively when it first presents. This is a baffling omission on the part of the NHS, which still recommends that most anorexics be treated 'on an outpatient basis'. It is also a damning indictment of a culture that persistently fails to take the emotional distress of young adults, and particularly young women, seriously.

Anorexia is not a fashion statement or a lifestyle choice, but a psychological breakdown that leads to physical collapse. We can no longer afford to ignore the subtlest and most deadly of mental illnesses.

11 March 2009

⇨ A lot of young people, many of whom are not overweight in the first place, want to be thinner. They often try to lose weight by dieting or skipping meals. For some, worries about weight becomes an obsession. This can turn into a serious eating disorder. (page 1)

⇨ Having anorexia means you think you are fat even when you are very thin. You often go to a lot of trouble to avoid eating. You may also make yourself throw up, take laxatives or spend hours exercising. (page 3)

⇨ Anorexia is a serious medical condition, not just a phase or a fad. (page 3)

⇨ In developed countries, around one in every 200 to 2 in every 200 young women have bulimia. Men can have bulimia too, but it's much more common in women. For every man who has the condition, there are around nine or ten women who have it. (page 4)

⇨ Binge eating is different from normal appetite increases or overeating from time to time. People with a binge eating problem eat unusually large amounts of food on a regular basis. (page 6)

⇨ A survey of 600 young people by beat has discovered that out of those surveyed, 91% had experienced bullying and 46% felt it contributed to their eating disorder. (page 8)

⇨ Eating disorder charities are reporting a rise in the number of people suffering from a serious psychological condition characterised by an obsession with healthy eating. (page 9)

⇨ Research from the NHS Information Centre (NHS IC) found that 6.4 per cent of adults had a problem with food, a figure much higher than previously thought. (page 11)

⇨ A survey by Girlguiding UK found that 12 per cent of 10- to 11-year-old girls wish to make themselves thinner. 21 per cent of 11- to 16-year-olds and 33 per cent of 16- to 21-year-olds would also like to be thinner. (page 17)

⇨ Research commissioned by Central YMCA, the UK's leading activity for health charity, revealed that 90 per cent of people believe the media and advertising industry should use models with a broader range of body sizes. (page 19)

⇨ Many girls say their mother has the biggest influence on their own self-image and they feel damaged by the effects of their mum's dieting and views on food. (page 20)

⇨ Dr John Morgan, a consultant psychiatrist and director of the Yorkshire Centre for Eating Disorders in Leeds, has found that growing numbers of young men are increasingly dissatisfied with their bodies. (page 21)

⇨ 26 per cent of 14- and 15-year-olds often don't eat breakfast, 22 per cent skip lunch and ten per cent regularly go without either, a study by the Schools Health Education Unit has found. (page 22)

⇨ A new report by Dr Helga Dittmar and experts in the field of body image has detailed scientific evidence on how the use of airbrushing to promote body-perfect ideals in advertising is causing problems in young women. These include eating disorders, depression, extreme exercising and encouraging cosmetic surgery. (page 23)

⇨ The Royal College of Psychiatrists has called for the Government must do more to address the dangers of pro-eating disorder websites and keep young people safe online. (page 25)

⇨ A major new study suggests that thousands of girls are predisposed to develop anorexia because of the way their brains developed in the womb. (page 28)

⇨ Talking therapies are often an important part of eating disorder treatments and may include: counselling, cognitive behaviour therapy (CBT), interpersonal therapy (IPT), group therapy and family therapy. (page 29)

⇨ John Evans, a professor of sociology at Loughborough University, has carried out research on the impact of anti-obesity campaigns on adolescents which showed that it could inadvertently lead to more concern about their weight and potentially propel them towards a damaging relationship with food. (page 33)

⇨ According to a survey by beat, only 15% of people felt their GP understood eating disorders and knew how to help. (page 36)

⇨ Wellcome Trust researchers have developed a new 'enhanced' form of cognitive behavioural therapy (CBT-E) that has been shown to have the potential to treat more than eight out of ten cases of eating disorders in adults. (page 37)

⇨ Anorexia has the highest mortality rate of any mental illness, but it remains one of the least understood. It is estimated that between 8% and 20% of sufferers will die as a result of the condition – half of them by suicide – and that a further 30% will remain ill for life, with complications including osteoporosis, digestive diseases, chronic anxiety, psychosis and heart failure. (page 38)

GLOSSARY

Anorexia nervosa

If you have anorexia, you're very underweight and you dread being fat. Having anorexia means you think you are fat even when you are very thin. You often go to a lot of trouble to avoid eating. You may also make yourself throw up, take laxatives or spend hours exercising.

Body dysmorphic disorder (BDD)

People with BDD are preoccupied or obsessed with defects in their appearance, either real or imagined. The obsession can focus on any part of the body, but the most common are on the face or head, specifically the skin, hair and nose.

Body image

Your body image is your mental picture of the way you look. How you think about your body relates to how you think about yourself as a whole, so a negative body image is often linked to low self-esteem and can lead to anxiety and depression.

Binge eating

Binge eating is when a person eats large amounts of food in one go, and feels out of control and unable to stop. It can be a symptom of the other eating disorders such as bulimia nervosa or anorexia nervosa. The difference is that people with binge eating disorder do not vomit or use laxatives or starve themselves in between binges to compensate for the extra food they have eaten, and so are very likely to gain weight.

Bulimia nervosa

If you have bulimia, you worry about putting on weight, but you sometimes lose control and eat huge amounts of food. Afterwards you might make yourself sick, take medicines such as laxatives or water pills, or exercise intensely so as not to gain weight. You keep all of this secret, and you might feel ashamed and guilty.

Cosmetic surgery

Cosmetic or aesthetic surgery refers to a non-essential surgical procedure to improve one's appearance.

'Drunkorexic'

A 'drunkorexic' is someone who skips meals so they can binge drink without putting on weight.

Eating disorders

Eating disorders are a group of mental health disorders that interfere with normal eating habits. They can lead to serious health problems and, in the case of both bulimia nervosa and anorexia nervosa, even death. Individuals suffering from an eating disorder often have a distorted body image.

Eating Disorder Not Otherwise Specified (ED-NOS)

Individuals with disordered eating patterns who do not meet some of the essential diagnostic criteria for specific disorders like anorexia and bulimia may be diagnosed with ED-NOS.

Obesity

Obesity is a condition which occurs when, due to the accumulation of excess body fat, an individual becomes severely overweight and their BMI exceeds 30. Obesity can cause serious health problems and increases the risk of developing diseases such as heart disease, diabetes and some types of cancer.

Orthorexia nervosa

A recently-recognised psychological condition characterised by an obsession with healthy eating.

Overweight

A person is considered overweight if their BMI is between 25 and 30. According to government statistics, one in four men and one in three women in the UK are overweight.

Pro-eating disorder websites

'Pro-ana' (pro-anorexia) and 'pro-mia' (pro-bulimia) websites are online communities which those suffering from an eating disorder may visit for friendship and support. However, such sites can be harmful as sufferers may share information on how to lose weight or tips on maintaining and hiding eating disorders. Some sites discuss eating disorders as a lifestyle choice rather than a disorder and there are concerns that they encourage vulnerable people who visit them to sustain a pattern of damaging behaviour.

Self-esteem

The word 'esteem' is derived from the Latin word which means 'to estimate'. Self-esteem can be described as the way we view ourselves, how we value ourselves or how much we like ourselves.

Size zero

Size zero refers to a UK size four (size zero in the US) and is often referred to in the debate surrounding extreme thinness. Some fashion shows have now banned size zero models from the catwalk to counter claims that they are bad role models for young people and could be responsible for a rise in eating disorders.

INDEX

Additional Resources

Other Issues titles

If you are interested in researching further some of the issues raised in *Understanding Eating Disorders* you may like to read the following titles in the **Issues** series:

⇨ Vol. 176 *Health Issues for Young People* (ISBN 978 1 86168 500 1)

⇨ Vol. 170 *Body Image and Self-Esteem* (ISBN 978 1 86168 484 4)

⇨ Vol. 165 *Bullying Issues* (ISBN 978 1 86168 469 1)

⇨ Vol. 162 *Staying Fit* (ISBN 978 1 86168 455 4)

⇨ Vol. 158 *The Internet Revolution* (ISBN 978 1 86168 451 6)

⇨ Vol. 142 *Media Issues* (ISBN 978 1 86168 408 0)

⇨ Vol. 141 *Mental Health* (ISBN 978 1 86168 407 3)

⇨ Vol. 136 *Self-Harm* (ISBN 978 1 86168 388 5)

⇨ Vol. 125 *Understanding Depression* (ISBN 978 1 86168 364 9)

⇨ Vol. 88 *Food and Nutrition* (ISBN 978 1 86168 289 5)

For more information about these titles, visit our website at www.independence.co.uk/publicationslist

Useful organisations

You may find the websites of the following organisations useful for further research:

⇨ **Anorexia and Bulimia Care (ABC):** www.anorexiabulimiacare.co.uk

⇨ **British Medical Journal:** www.bmj.com

⇨ **Central YMCA:** www.ymca.co.uk

⇨ **Children First for Health:** www.childrenfirst.nhs.uk

⇨ **Girlguiding UK:** www.girlguiding.org.uk

⇨ **Health Service Journal:** www.hsj.co.uk

⇨ **Institute of Psychiatry:** www.iop.kcl.ac.uk

⇨ **Men Get Eating Disorders Too:** www.mengetedstoo.co.uk

⇨ **Rethink:** www.rethink.org

⇨ **Royal College of Psychiatrists:** www.rcpsych.ac.uk

⇨ **Samaritans:** www.samaritans.org

⇨ **Sane:** www.sane.org.uk

ACKNOWLEDGEMENTS

The publisher is grateful for permission to reproduce the following material.

While every care has been taken to trace and acknowledge copyright, the publisher tenders its apology for any accidental infringement or where copyright has proved untraceable. The publisher would be pleased to come to a suitable arrangement in any such case with the rightful owner.

Chapter One: Eating Disorders

Eating disorders in young people, © Royal College of Psychiatrists, *Anorexia*, © BMJ Publishing Group Limited ('BMJ Group') 2009, *Bulimia*, © BMJ Publishing Group Limited ('BMJ Group') 2009, *Binge eating*, © Great Ormond Street Hospital 2009, *Other eating disorders*, © Institute of Psychiatry, *Bullying and eating disorders*, © beat, *Healthy food obsession sparks rise in new disorder*, © Guardian News & Media Ltd 2009, *Do we all have disordered eating?*, © Psychologies, *The rise of male eating disorders*, © Samaritans, *Size zero bad news for bones*, © University of Bristol, *Some facts*, © Men Get Eating Disorders Too, *Eating disorders over 40*, © Scotsman, *Are you a drunkorexic?*, © Drinkaware.

Chapter Two: Body Image and Media

Girls' attitudes, © Girlguiding UK, *Anxiety over body image*, Central YMCA, *Girls 'damaged' by mum's diet*, © Press Association, *'Crisis in masculinity' leads to eating disorders*, © Royal College of Psychiatrists, *Living on one meal a day*, © Associated Newspapers Ltd, *Airbrushed ads damaging a generation of young women*, © University of Sussex, *Size zero: an undernourished argument*, © Telegraph Media Group, *The fashion industry*, © Binge Eating Disorder Association, *Moss criticised for 'pro-anorexia comment'*, © Adfero, *Psychiatrists urge action to tackle 'pro-ana' websites*, © Royal College of Psychiatrists, *Pro-eating disorder websites*, © SANE, *Too fat to be a princess?*, © British Psychological Society, *Anorexia risk 'could be predicted'*, © Guardian News & Media Ltd 2009.

Chapter Three: Recovery

What are the treatments for eating disorders?, © Rethink, *Eating disorders in teenagers*, © Anorexia and Bulimia Care (ABC), *Self-help tips*, © Disordered Eating, *Obesity leaves eating disorders in the shade*, © Health Service Journal, *'While I was eating I would go into a trance'*, © NHS Choices, *Choice or chance?*, © beat, *Psychotherapy for eating disorders*, © Wellcome Trust, *An aching hunger*, © Guardian News & Media Ltd 2009.

Photographs

Stock Xchng: pages 3 (Asif Akbar); 4 (mokra); 13 (Amir Darafsheh); 15 (Stephanie Berghaeuser); 16 (Carlos Zaragoza); 27 (hyle zacharias); 30 (Laura Glover); 31 (sanja gjenero); 37 (trinamole).

Illustrations

Pages 1, 10, 17, 32: Don Hatcher; pages 5, 21, 26, 34: Simon Kneebone; pages 6, 25: Bev Aisbett; pages 9, 14, 29, 39: Angelo Madrid.

Editorial and layout by Claire Owen, on behalf of Independence Educational Publishers.

And with thanks to the team: Mary Chapman, Sandra Dennis, Claire Owen and Jan Sunderland.

Lisa Firth
Cambridge
January, 2010